CHIC BOUTIQUERS AT HOME

INTERIORS INSPIRATION AND EXPERT
ADVICE FROM CREATIVE ONLINE SELLERS

ELLIE TENNANT

photography by JAMES GARDINER

RYLAND PETERS & SMALL

LONDON • NEW YORK

Senior Designer
Megan Smith
Commissioning Editor
Stephanie Milner
Head of Production
Patricia Harrington
Production
David Hearn
Art Director
Leslie Harrington
Editorial Director
Julia Charles
Publisher
Cindy Richards

Indexer
Vanessa Bird

First published in 2015 by
Ryland Peters & Small
20–21 Jockey's Fields,
London WC1R 4BW
and
341 E 116th St
New York, NY 10029
www.rylandpeters.com

Text © Ellie Tennant 2015

Design and photographs ©
Ryland Peters & Small 2015

ISBN: 978-1-84975-664-8

Printed and bound in China

10 9 8 7 6 5 4 3 2 1

A CIP record for this
book is available from the
British Library. US Library
of Congress Cataloging-in-
Publication Data has been
applied for.

CONTENTS

INTRODUCTION

Online shopping is the future. Consumer trend forecasters from Future Foundation report that 80 per cent of UK adults now buy online and, by 2020, 90 per cent will be engaging in e-commerce.

Not only are we shopping online more, we're changing how we do it, too, as we migrate from desktop computers and laptops to smart phones and tablet devices. Now, we can shop for our homes and lives wherever we want, whenever we want.

Without the expenses of a bricks-and-mortar shop, smaller independent brands can set up and start trading with ease, giving us access to a wider range of chic boutiques than ever before. The growth of online shopping also means that we can buy from brands that are based abroad – many of which have introduced international shipping at competitive prices to attract a global customer base.

But what is a 'chic boutiquer'? Who are these fashion-forward, online style gurus? And is 'boutiquers' even a word? Well, no, not really, but it is now. (And it sounds catchier than 'online shop owners'!).

'Chic' is harder to define. According to *The Oxford English Dictionary*, it means: 'elegantly and stylishly fashionable', which of course, accurately describes the online sellers in this book. But somehow, this definition doesn't seem enough to encapsulate the talent that the inspirational people I have met during the making of this book embody.

The word 'chic' is thought to have a German origin, from the Middle Ages word 'schick', which means 'skill'. We're getting closer here. Trends come and go, but what these e-tailers have is a timeless sense of style – unique, creative and impressive – not limited by the fickle flow and ebb of fashion. These people are driven by something much deeper. They all have the ability to tap into an internal pool of creativity and, as a result,

their homes and online shops offer a wealth of inspiration that far transcends what's new or what's cool. Now, that's skill.

My own definition of 'chic' has been enhanced and enriched by the homes, boutiques and lives I've had the pleasure of exploring for this book.

At Sian Tucker of fforest general stores' coastal Welsh cottage, it was her amazing collection of hand-carved wooden spoons that struck me as particularly chic, as well as the way she had let a tiny leaf of ivy live, unharmed, in her shower room after it had somehow managed to penetrate the thick slate walls. At Mini Moderns owners Keith Stephenson and Mark Hampshire's Dungeness home, it was the care with which they had excavated and celebrated the original features of their railway carriage that left an impression on me. Thrifty Jeska and Dean Hearne, who run The Future Kept from Hastings, showed me that living a more sustainable life is definitely chic.

My understanding of the word continued to expand with every creative seller I encountered. In New York, the simple feather and leather decoration that Japanese crafter Asumi Tomita gave me seemed to sum up the word 'chic' beautifully; fuss-free, serene and handmade from natural materials. The Brooklyn creatives I met all had 'chic' skills – from painter Helen Dealtry's amazing ability to convey the essence of flowers with a few brushstrokes to Australian weaver Maryanne Moodie's innate talent for playing with colours and textures, and ceramicist Elaine Tian's knack for hand-crafting tiny, ceramic bowls that resemble seascapes, awash with watery glazes.

In Scandinavia, Ylva Skarp's Swedish family home was the perfect balance of sleekness and warmth, while Danish designer Rebecca Uth in Copenhagen expertly combined rustic finds with cutting-edge, contemporary pieces to create a warm home. Copenhagen-based designer Kristina Dam was a master of refined, restrained design and a whizz at creating long-lasting pieces that would look good for lifetimes to come. Meanwhile, in the Netherlands, Janneke van Houtum had created magical storyland bedrooms for her two sons, better than any stylist could conjure up, thanks to the love and care she had put into them. Dutch blogger Danielle de Lange had a very beautiful, vintage, Moroccan rug that her newly adopted rescue dog Lola was in the habit of destroying. 'It has to go!' she said (meaning the rug, not the dog!), for, in the 'chicest' of spaces, life and love always take priority and the interior is more beautiful as a result.

I think my definition of what's not chic was also enhanced by this project. Inspired and energized by the small business owners I met, I was dismayed to hear from Helen about the Starbucks in Brooklyn that has disguised itself as an independent café in a desperate attempt to 'blend in'. And I was saddened to hear from Jeska and Dean that a UK supermarket has started to sell 'artisanal' coffee in brown paper bags. But I was heartened to learn that authenticity equals power. The big boys can attempt to imitate the real thing, but they can never succeed.

Small businesses tend to be more original, ethical and interesting. Let's support them by shopping from them whenever we can, from small retailers we know and we know we can trust, for durable, long-lasting, well-made products with ethical origins.

That's pretty darn chic.

DESIGNERS

Artistic online sellers who design
their own exclusive product ranges

THE LONELINESS OF THE LONG DISTANCE RUNNER   Alan Sillitoe

Georgy Girl   Margaret Forster

UP THE JUNCTION   Nell Dunn

CITY OF SPADES   COLIN MACINNES

THE SUBTERRANEANS   JACK KEROUAC

A Summer Place   Sloan Wilson

TO SIR, WITH LOVE   E. R. BRAITHWAITE

SATURDAY NIGHT AND SUNDAY MORNING   Sillitoe

Midnight Cowboy   James Leo Herlihy   Panther

SHIPS

WARNE

THIS PAGE Mark and Keith display their collection of Portmeirion's 'Totem' tableware (by Susan Williams-Ellis, 1963) on a vintage luggage rack, reclaimed from the London Underground Metropolitan line and sold at the London Transport Museum. The table is an eBay find.

OPPOSITE Although it looks like an expensive, bespoke design, the compact, freestanding kitchen is actually from IKEA. 'It was great value for money. Our clever builder adapted and customized the units to fit our small space perfectly,' says Mark.

MINI MODERNS

www.minimoderns.com

Dungeness is the only official desert in the UK. It's a strange, surreal, beautiful place, where sky, sea and vast expanses of shingle meet the surrounding land. Here, nestled between clumps of grass on the sands, is a converted railway carriage/railroad car that belongs to designers Mark Hampshire and Keith Stephenson – the duo behind the online boutique Mini Moderns.

FACT FILE /
MINI MODERNS

CHIC BOUTIQUERS
Mark Hampshire and
Keith Stephenson

BASED
London and Dungeness, UK

ONLINE SHOP
Mini Moderns

ADDRESS
www.minimoderns.com

LAUNCHED
2006

STOCK
Wallpapers, lampshades,
paints and home accessories

SHOP STYLE
Retro, colourful, inspiring

HOME
A converted railway
carriage/railroad car
that has a mid-century
modern interior with
a contemporary twist

LEFT The kitchen is airy and light, thanks to the original carriage windows. Colourful kitchenalia designed by the duo makes for a striking display. 'We collect vintage Scandinavian enamelware by Cathrineholm, so we enjoyed designing our own range,' says Keith. Their cheery creations look at home beside more Portmeirion 'Totem' pieces.

The land surrounding Mark and Keith's Dungeness home is almost unfeasibly flat and empty. The only interruptions on the horizon are two lighthouses, a handful of cabins and fishermen's huts, the odd passing ship in the distance and an enormous, unmissable nuclear power plant, which dominates the landscape in an eerie but rather splendid way – especially at night, when distant foghorns sound and the bright light of the huge building spills out across the mist-covered plains and marshy waters.

'We'd been visiting this area for 17 years before we bought our home here,' says Mark. 'The strange oddness of Dungeness really appeals to us – even on cold, wintery days,' he adds.

'It's bleak, yes,' agrees Keith, '...but that's why we love it. Dungeness is hard to describe – it's other-worldly and unique. Everything here adds to the atmosphere, from the rusty, disintegrating fishing huts on the beach to the shingle that reflects light upwards and gives an unusual aura.' The landscape might appear to be barren, but on closer inspection, it is teeming with life – the lakes are home to birds and the unusual climate means that

vegetation thrives. 'There's a weird harmony here,' explains Keith. 'The nuclear power station shields the windswept shingle, so rare species can survive.'

When the railway closed down, local people were given the opportunity to buy the old carriages and relocate them to the beach, to use as angling huts and holiday homes. Keith and Mark dreamed of owning one, but received mixed messages from local residents.

'Dungeness is constantly shrouded in myth,' says Keith. 'Nothing is straightforward. Even simple processes disappear into a whirl of mythology!'

Mark agrees. 'Ten years ago, we overheard somebody say that you couldn't buy property in Dungeness unless you were born and bred there. We soon found out that wasn't the case.'

In 2012, they spotted a carriage for sale and fell in love with it instantly. 'We saw it on a Sunday and put in an offer on Monday,' remembers Mark. 'It was dark inside, but we could see it had incredible potential.' The main building was sound, but there were leaks in the roof and a lot of basic work needed to be done before decoration could commence.

'It's basically a shed on an exposed beach and the climate here is harsh – if you don't keep on top of maintenance, nature will win,' explains Keith. 'It had been on the market for 18 months and had already drastically deteriorated in that time,' adds Mark.

During the renovation process, the couple discovered 1920s tongue-and-groove panelling and the original carriage doors, which now provide a focal point in the living room. 'It was like an excavation,' chuckles Keith. 'Everything was covered up with cladding and boards. We spent three months uncovering character. It was a long process, but we really got to know the building.'

The energetic couple painted walls white, restored floorboards and fitted a wood-burning stove. Because their railway carriage was originally a guard's van, it had a glass skylight – or lantern – that the guard would have looked out of. 'We noticed the glass box in the ceiling when we viewed the property, but it didn't let in much light because it was covered with a Perspex case, which was opaque and sand-blasted,' explains Keith. 'As soon as we removed the plastic box, the whole room was flooded with light and we suddenly realized how lucky we were to have such an unusual feature.'

Having a coastal retreat has influenced Mark and Keith's designs, which grace wallpaper, fabric and home accessories. 'We like to use our beach house

TOP RIGHT On the wall are fascinating old photos of the carriage. 'They were here when we moved in,' explains Mark. 'The grandchildren of the man who originally put the carriage on the beach popped in to visit once. It was nice to hear about the happy family holidays they had here.'

RIGHT This 'P.L.U.T.O' cushion by Mini Moderns features circular motifs based on the 'sound mirrors' at Dungeness that are close to the carriage, at Denge. 'The background of this pattern is inspired by "dazzle" camouflage, used on military vessels,' adds Mark. Every shape has a meaning.

THIS PAGE The living room is bright and airy, with panoramic views of the sea. 'I found the Guy Rogers sofa and armchairs on eBay,' says Keith. 'They're upholstered in original Harris tweed wool fabric. Vintage furniture works best here – it has small proportions and you can see floor underneath each piece, which makes the room look bigger than it really is.'

STYLE TIP
White walls reflect light for a spacious look, but be sure to introduce plenty of warm, natural wood elements to prevent the room from feeling cold.

as a showcase for our products,' says Mark. 'We always say, if we can't live with our designs, we shouldn't produce them. Our benchmark is always: would we have this in our own home?'

The surreal and rugged local landscape formed the basis for the 'Hinterland' collection – a range that includes shingle-patterned linen fabrics featuring lighthouses and huts, and a new 'P.L.U.T.O.' wallpaper design, inspired by the 'Pipe Line Under The Ocean', a World War II fuel line built under the English Channel from Dungeness to France, to supply the D-Day invasion troops with fuel. 'The design also

features curved motifs based on the Dungeness sound mirrors, also known as "listening ears". They're pre-radar military devices,' says Mark.

Their attention to detail when curating collections and putting together new prints is incredible. 'We're not just pattern-makers,' says Keith. 'We'd find it really boring if we were. We worked in branding before launching Mini Moderns, so we like to create designs that tell stories and take people on a journey through a range.'

Often, a design begins life in one context and ends it in another, as with their striking 'Pavilion' print, inspired by the Abacus screen at the Festival of Britain, but equally reminiscent of seaside buoys. 'We stick to a strict colour palette and add new colours gradually and thoughtfully, so all our designs work together,' explains Mark.

Informed by the past, Keith and Mark find unending inspiration in 1950s and 1960s designs, and have been fans of the mid-century era ever since they were teenagers buying second-hand clothing in charity/thrift shops. Nowadays, the vintage shops in nearby Rye provide a rich hunting ground for the eagle-eyed pair. 'We love to potter around,' says Keith. 'We visit the antiques shops, then come home and walk on the beach. We never take our computers to Dungeness – there's no TV and no wifi. We think, we create and we plan our next set of stories. Until you have space, you don't realize how much you need it.'

'We saw it on a Sunday and put in an offer on Monday,' Mark remembers. 'The carriage was dark inside, but we could see it had incredible potential.'

ABOVE The bedroom provides the perfect place to showcase one of the Mini Moderns wallpapers, 'Backgammon', inspired by the game's discs and triangles. The 1960s chair was a gift from a friend. The linen cushion on the chair features 'Dungeness' – a pattern inspired by the local area, featuring the lighthouse and a rusty anchor.

OPPOSITE The stunning G Plan 'Fresco' bed (another eBay find) was much too bulky for the compact bedroom. 'I ended up trimming a little bit of wood off each of the bedside table legs to make the whole frame lower,' Mark chuckles. The 'Fresh Local Fish' print is inspired by a nearby sign and features on designs in their online shop, too.

THIS PAGE The duo's stylish home office is decorated with 'Paisley Crescent' wallpaper, from 'The Buddha of Suburbia' collection by Mini Moderns. Vintage accessories complete the look.
OPPOSITE FROM TOP LEFT Blues and books in the bedroom alcove; an old gardening sieve fixed to the wall provides a chic cubbyhole; the airy bathroom is decorated with 'Darjeeling' wallpaper by Mini Moderns.

MARK AND KEITH LOVE:
• Hopper and Space: www.hopperandspace.com
• Present & Correct: www.presentandcorrect.com
• Fears and Khan: www.fearsandkahn.co.uk

TOP E-TAILING TIPS:
• Act on what you stand for. You can't tell people you're funny – you have to make them laugh!

• It's important to connect on Twitter, Facebook and so on – when you're setting up, consider what kind of brand you want to be. We are very personal, approachable and friendly as a brand, so we get involved heavily with social media. Otherwise, our brand values mean nothing.

• Storytelling is important – if customers are interested in the stories behind your designs, they become more interested in your brand as a whole.

• Meet your customers face to face when you can. Pop-up shops, studio sales and events are a great way to interact offline.

KRISTINA DAM STUDIO

www.kristinadam.dk

From her airy Copenhagen apartment, designer Kristina Dam is busy putting her architecture training to good use, building her own design 'universe' online. Her fashion-forward products are functional yet warm – her aesthetic is Nordic, but never cold. Kristina's home and shop are both effortlessly chic, filled with designer finds and fresh ideas.

Kristina Dam is an inspiration to all hard-working, self-employed mothers. She calmly juggles breast-feeding with answering emails and taking orders – her flat is an unlikely haven of tranquillity, somehow, despite the fact that she has a toddler, a four-month-old baby and a thriving business that's rapidly expanding.

'I advise people to take the first two months off work after having a baby,' she says, '…because I only had a few days and it was really exhausting.' You'd never guess – she is impressively cool and collected, seemingly unflappable. Her online shop as well as her home reflect her personality: organized, fuss-free, restrained.

'In 2000, I studied at art school for four months, learning drawing skills and honing perspective and precision,' says Kristina, a talented paper artist and illustrator. 'I wanted to be a graphic designer, so I went on to do a design degree with emphasis on graphic design at the School of Architecture and Design at the Royal Danish School of Fine Arts,' she says. 'My experience in architecture influences me a lot. I learned a lot about space and perspective, and learned to draw and also how to make things. I understand what it's possible to achieve and have a thorough knowledge of the manufacturing process. I love to use a variety of materials and dip into lots of different areas. Wood, blackened steel, marble, brass…'

Kristina's products, from artworks and textiles to sculptures and pieces of furniture, are a seamless blend of geometry and art. Here, clean edges, strong shapes and minimal linear designs dominate.

ABOVE Kristina's stylish living room is a shrine to Scandinavian design: the wooden task lamp is by Muuto, the cushions are the result of a collaboration between Kristina and Danish brand by Lassen, the coffee table is by Hay and the hexagonal patterned blanket is by Ferm Living. The stunning collages are original art pieces by Kristina. 'My art is fluid and layered, so quite different from a lot of my design work,' says Kristina. 'In my interior universe, my colour palette is Nordic, but in my paintings I like to use a lot of different colours.'

FACT FILE / KRISTINA DAM STUDIO

CHIC BOUTIQUER
Kristina Dam
BASED
Copenhagen, Denmark
ONLINE SHOP
Kristina Dam Studio
ADDRESS
www.kristinadam.dk or
www.kristinadam.bigcartel.com
LAUNCHED
2012

STOCK
Original art, prints, home textiles,
furniture and accessories
SHOP STYLE
Graphic, architectural,
contemporary
HOME
A spacious apartment in central
Copenhagen, with period
features, designer furniture
and vintage finds

THIS PAGE Kristina spotted her vintage day bed at a flea market. 'I wanted it so badly,' she recalls. 'I was six months pregnant, but carried it all the way home! I painted the base black and now it looks really cool.' The black leather chair is by Poul Kjærholm.

After graduating in 2007, Kristina spent five years working as a graphic designer in a big studio. 'I learned so much, but I had the feeling that I needed to do my own thing, so in 2012 I set up my own company.'

She started by focusing on her original artworks and illustration prints, then expanded into other areas such as textiles, furniture and ornamental sculptures. All of Kristina's products have a simple, Nordic feel. 'I like to work with natural materials like oak,' she explains. 'The most important thing for me is that my designs challenge people to be bold and experimental in their homes. All my products have a twist – nothing is ordinary.'

Her elegant marble-topped side table design, for example, has two uses – the top can be moved to the bottom and the table base becomes a 3D frame for a piece of sculpture; her pared-back magazine holder has a removable marble plate on top – the perfect perch for a coffee cup – so it doubles up as a small side table, too; Kristina's beautiful wall mirror isn't a simple circle – it's a wall sculpture with 2D and 3D elements; functional art.

'My goal is to create my own universe,' reveals Kristina with impressive resolve. 'I'm planning to introduce vases and glass candlesticks soon. I constantly strive to move forward.'

In just three years, Kristina's work has received a lot of attention. She's currently collaborating with an Istanbul-based design studio (Gaia & Gino) for the Wallpaper* Handmade installation in Milan and, thanks to a legion of admirers around the world, her sales have increased so much that she can now no longer store all her stock at home and needs to use a warehouse and employ a professional packaging and shipping firm. Her customers are drawn to the cutting-edge designs Kristina produces, which feel at once timelessly stylish yet modern and ultra cool.

ABOVE FROM TOP LEFT Kristina's leather chair is by Danish designer Børge Mogensen and the floor lamp is by Arne Jacobsen – 'I love having a dark wall to position shapely, white pieces against,' says Kristina; the white coffee table by Hay is the perfect place for Kristina to display her brass geometric shapes and marble trivets; a sculptural wooden cube hangs on the dark grey living room wall. 'I like the spectacular contrast between light and dark.'

So what inspires Kristina's fresh Danish designs and how is she able to consistently predict 'the next big thing' in so many different areas? 'It's important to go out, see the world, travel to other cities, visit exhibitions, and then you can find ideas all around you,' she reveals. 'I often get inspired when I am abroad – I love cities such as London, Bangkok, Berlin and New York.'

Kristina's ability to tap into the fashion world helps her to keep her finger on the pulse. 'The fashion industry is often a step ahead of interior design in terms of colours and materials, so I keep abreast of fashion design, too. My brother owns a clothing company and I occasionally design for him, so that helps to keep my ideas fresh,' she explains.

The Copenhagen apartment that Kristina shares with her husband Ketil and their two young children is the perfect space for Kristina to showcase her work and for her to experiment with art and display. 'We moved here in 2008,' she says. 'We loved the big windows and the way that daylight floods in. The rooms are nice and big, so we have plenty of space, too, which is great.'

Kristina's collection of designer pieces from the likes of Tom Dixon, Hay, Flos, Ferm Living and Arne Jacobsen, combined with her innate ability to expertly style every corner, means her home could easily grace the pages of a glossy magazine,

TOP LEFT Homemade fruit liqueurs, made by Ketil and neatly labelled with luggage tags, line a kitchen alcove. 'My parents have a "summer house" in Skagen,' says Kristina. 'The landscape is beautiful and we always gather lots of berries.'

LEFT Kristina likes the contrast of the old original tiles with her sleek, new kitchen. The wooden stool belonged to her grandfather, who was a shopkeeper. 'He stood on it to reach high shelves, so it reminds me of him,' she says.

THIS PAGE The kitchen table is a 1960s design, bought from a flea market. The copper pendant light is by Tom Dixon. 'When we moved in, the floorboards were tatty and worn. We painted them white to smarten them up and maximize light,' explains Kristina.

'The suspended cot is by Leander.
I think it's really cool and I love
the design, but our baby doesn't
like to sleep in it!'

OPPOSITE Clutter-free and minimalist, the bedroom is a haven of tranquillity with large windows overlooking trees. The floor lamp is by Castiglioni, from Flos, while the quilted geometric bed cover was designed by Kristina and is available in her shop. THIS PAGE A simple metal pole and two leather belts create a striking hanging wardrobe/closet. Ketil collects old aeroplane models – he found these ones on eBay and displays them propped up in a corner. Whitewashed floorboards enhance the feeling of space in the light room.

STYLE TIP
Create a nursery corner with vintage, wooden toys and designer furniture. A changing mat on a chest of drawers provides a temporary changing station.

LEFT Multi-tasking mother Kristina has cleverly adapted a corner of her home studio into a temporary changing station. White-washed floorboards and monochrome accessories create a stylish feel. OPPOSITE FROM TOP LEFT Colourful cushions in the bedroom warm up the Nordic interior; Kristina's favourite chair is this vintage woven string one by Hans Wegner; the geometric paper shapes were designed to be Christmas tree decorations, but Kristina has turned them into a mobile for her baby.

yet, thankfully, with quirky, vintage flea-market finds and her own-brand creations in every room, the overall look is anything but staged. It's perfection, but an appealing, 'real' version of perfection – a cleverly curated home that looks stunning but is a joy to live in, too.

The kitchen is Kristina's favourite room. 'It's the place where we always hang out if we have friends over,' she says. 'We're lucky that it's very light and I grow potted herbs and flowers on the balcony outside.'

If de-cluttering seems like a chore, take inspiration from Kristina's pared-back look. Her home is the epitome of William Morris's adage that everything should be beautiful or useful. The rooms aren't sparse, but she has achieved that magical perfect balance of 'space' and 'stuff', allowing her carefully chosen possessions to breathe and be admired. Her approach to design – both at home and at work – is not only brilliant, it's brilliantly useful.

KRISTINA LOVES:
- Elkeland: www.elkeland.bigcartel.com
- The Minimalist: www.theminimalist.com.au
- The Poster Club: www.theposterclub.com

TOP E-TAILING TIPS:
- Start small and keep your stock at home, but take it step by step and be aware that you will need a bigger space at some time. Make a plan.

- Choose an easy-to-use platform such as Big Cartel. It's simple to make a webshop that looks good using straightforward design templates, and the template shops all hook up with PayPal.

- Ensure you use a platform that allows you to edit and update your shop yourself. I like Big Cartel because it's easy to upload new products.

- Keep moving forward. That's important. I started out with art prints, but so many artists sell art prints now. That's partly why I've expanded into furniture, textiles and sculptures.

THIS PAGE 'The oil painting is by an artist called Victor Wang,' says Helen. 'He paints with oils on top of Chinese manuscripts and creates fascinating collaged layers.' The pendant lamp is by &Tradition.

OPPOSITE The fireplace was disused and in bad shape when the couple moved in, so they decided to fit shelves inside the chimney breast. 'This is a nice corner to curl up in with a book,' says Helen.

DEALTRY

www.helendealtry.com

In a quiet street in south-side Williamsburg, Brooklyn, is a smart townhouse. A sympathetic restoration has transformed this formerly unloved building into a stunning home and now the interior is a perfect blend of old and new, with sleek lines and natural textures. It is home to English artist and designer Helen Dealtry, her American partner Dan Barry and their cheeky rescue dog Dudley.

FACT FILE / DEALTRY

CHIC BOUTIQUER
Helen Dealtry
BASED
New York, USA
ONLINE SHOP
Dealtry
ADDRESS
www.helendealtry.com
LAUNCHED
2012
STOCK
Cashmere/modal scarves
and watercolour paintings
SHOP STYLE
Textural, linear, layered
HOME
A Williamsburg townhouse
with exposed brickwork and
a completely renovated,
high-spec interior

LEFT Exposed brick walls give the office area a warm, industrial feel. 'Dan bought the canvases from a street vendor when he first moved to New York. He found the vintage desk in Arizona, where there is loads of affordable mid-century furniture,' reveals Helen. The chair is an Eames reproduction.

OPPOSITE On the wall of the living room hangs one of Helen's stunning scarves, 'Ohara', which was inspired by the disciplined Japanese art form of flower arranging: ikebana. 'I like to concentrate on a few key elements – as opposed to a big bunch of flowers, where everything gets lost,' explains Helen.

Having lived in New York for over a decade, Brit-abroad Helen Dealtry no longer feels like a tourist. 'America is my home now,' she says. 'I miss people in England, of course, and I'd love to be able to get back to the UK a bit more, but this is where my life is.'

The vibrancy of 'the city that never sleeps' has well and truly hooked Helen, who grew up in Woking, South East England. 'I love New York. It has an energy that I can't explain – it's unique. I sense it as soon as I step off the plane.'

As an entrepreneur with an online boutique, Helen also enjoys the enterprising spirit in the city.

'It's somewhere you can come to, whatever your nationality, wherever you're from – and be accepted pretty readily,' she explains. 'You can come here and make it. It's a competitive city, but people are happy to help each other. It's so dynamic.'

Helen moved to New York in 2000, after being offered a job as a junior designer by a fashion brand during her graduate show in the UK. 'I studied textile fashion at the Winchester School of Art and moved to America straight after,' she recalls. 'I did a three-month placement, then returned to the UK for a brief stint, but couldn't resist New York for long! I came back and stayed

STYLE TIP
For a cohesive scheme
that looks harmonious,
use a 'colour trio'. Choose
a dominant colour in your
wall art, then find
cushions and flowers
that match.

'We did lots of research to keep the interior as authentic as possible. The tin-work ceiling tiles are the sort that would have originally been in a building of this era.'

at the same fashion studio, designing prints for womenswear and gradually worked my way up to become Creative Director.'

The work was intense, but great experience. Helen was expected to produce two designs a day, and fluid, hand-painted watercolour florals became her forte. 'When I first came to New York it was very stressful – I had to paint directly onto silk and there were some tears shed along the way. My painting skills have developed because I've worked on them so much.'

After a while, Helen wanted to branch out, so started to develop her own brand in 2009, producing elegant painterly cashmere/modal scarves. She launched her online shop to sell them to a wider audience a few years later and the fashion label Dealtry was born.

'It's nice to do my own thing finally,' she reveals. 'For years, I was designing clothes for other people, but now I'm developing patterns I would actually wear myself. I'm mixing florals with contemporary geometrics. It's fun, but it's a bit terrifying putting your name on a brand after working anonymously for so long.' Helen's colourful scarves are now highly sought after, and her original watercolour paintings are attracting attention, too, with exhibitions on the horizon and impressive sales. She is regularly commissioned to design for fashion brands and loves to collaborate with other creatives, such as ceramicist Re Jin Lee of Bailey Doesn't Bark.

Despite her tech-savvy shop and digital know-how, Helen's method is refreshingly old-fashioned. She hand-paints all her own designs, then manipulates them afterwards as required. Her studio is filled with the happy chaos of hands-on creativity – brushes, rags, piles of painted papers and palettes awash with swirling colours.

'When I'm painting, if I can get my hands on real flowers, then that's always my preference,' says Helen. 'Even just moving the vase a tiny bit gives you another angle to paint. You can get so much inspiration from a vase of flowers. The studio opposite mine is occupied by a floral designer who sometimes lets me borrow her beautiful blooms.'

OPPOSITE The spare bedroom retains original period features and is one of Helen's favourite rooms. 'It's a dark little hobbit hole where I can retreat to watch *Downton Abbey* on my laptop,' she laughs. 'It feels a bit cottage-y, with exposed brickwork, beautiful beams and a low ceiling. Somehow, it reminds me of England. I love it in there.'

Helen's studio is a mere 15-minute walk from the home she shares with her boyfriend Dan Barry, who bought the property in January 2011 and did an impressive 'gut renovation'. By October, the couple could move in and the previously dilapidated building was completely transformed.

'Structurally, we made some big changes,' explains Helen. 'We swapped the rooms around, moving the kitchen and living space upstairs and making it open plan, and we put the bedrooms and bathrooms downstairs where it's darker anyway.'

The couple worked with an architect to plan the layout and decided to remove the back wall of the house and replace it with floor-to-ceiling glass panels. 'Now the whole living space is flooded with light,' says Helen, happily.

Despite the contemporary additions, the couple didn't want to remove everything original from the house. 'We knew parts of the home would be clean and modern, so we wanted to retain some of the house's history,' says Helen. 'In the past, there had been a fire in the house, so there were some black soot marks on a wall, which we decided to leave rather than scrub them away. We exposed brick walls and beams, too, and tried to reinstate original features such as tin ceiling tiles.'

The end result is a powerful interior of contrasting elements – sleek, clean lines and cool, contemporary materials like

TOP Downstairs, Helen and Dan have blurred the boundaries between rooms. 'The bedroom, dressing area and wet room all have the same concrete floor – it unites the space,' says Helen. The curvaceous bathtub provides a focal point. **ABOVE** Helen's painterly artworks grace the walls of every room, providing cheery colour.

concrete and glass are softened and warmed up by the
natural textures of wood and brick.

Despite her love of the Big Apple, Helen relishes the
sanctuary her home provides from the hectic pace of city
living. 'If we moved out, the thing I'd miss most is the
huge magnolia tree in our garden,' she says. 'When we
first moved in, it didn't have any buds. I spent ages
trying to figure out what it was, from the shape of the

branches. In April, when we'd been here for six months,
the tree bloomed and it was amazing.'

The new huge glass windows blur the boundary
between the interior and the exterior. 'I love sitting on
the sofa, gazing outside,' adds Helen. 'Having a huge
window and a big green tree to admire is such a luxury
in New York. It's an intense place to live, so any bit of
private space is gold.'

HELEN LOVES:
- Spartan Shop: www.spartan-shop.com
- Modern Manor: www.modernmanorstore.com
- Vintage Martini: www.vintagemartini.com

TOP E-TAILING TIPS:

• Figure out your market first. Who are your customers? You need to know this before you can start.

• Your style and branding should be consistent throughout your online presence – on all social media platforms, for example.

• Find out what your customers want. Ask people for their feedback. It's always terrifying, but it's the only way to find out what you can improve on.

• I use Shopify and have a template that offers me a lot of freedom. I previously used a much more basic shop template, so experiment until you find the perfect fit. It takes time to get things right.

RO COLLECTION

www.rocollection.dk

After years working as design director for Georg Jensen, Danish creative Rebecca Uth decided to return to her roots and go it alone. Her new online boutique Ro Collection is a refreshing haven of serenity, longevity and authenticity in a world that's often dominated by flashy, fashion-fuelled, transient design. Rebecca's eclectic Copenhagen attic flat reflects her expert curation skills and demonstrates her natural flair for playing with contrasts while exercising restraint.

FACT FILE / RO COLLECTION

CHIC BOUTIQUER
Rebecca Uth
BASED
Copenhagen, Denmark
ONLINE SHOP
Ro Collection
ADDRESS
www.rocollection.dk
LAUNCHED
2014

STOCK
Fresh Danish designer creations that channel serene, simple elegance
SHOP STYLE
Global, hand-crafted, contrasting
HOME
A penthouse apartment in central Copenhagen, with exposed beams, raw cement walls and views across the rooftops

OPPOSITE A cabinet filled with curiosities picked up in Vietnam sits next to a rustic bench originally from France; 'The copper baskets I create for Ro were inspired by woven, natural designs,' reveals Rebecca.

THIS PAGE Rebecca was inspired to give her walls a cement finish after a trip to New York. 'My father helped to apply rough cement to the unfinished walls, leaving traces of the previous paints visible.'

STYLE TIP
Expose the beam framework within an old wall to create an open-plan space that feels open and spacious but is visually divided into distinct zones.

OPPOSITE The wooden beams that divide Rebecca's living and dining areas have original numbers and markings made by builders when they built the house. RIGHT 'Piano has always been my main instrument,' says Rebecca. 'I encouraged my two oldest children to play, but I've only had success with the youngest one – and I didn't push him at all!'

High above the rooftops of central Copenhagen, a mischievous ginger cat pads precariously along the windowsill of designer Rebecca Uth's stylish apartment. 'We just call him Kitty – he doesn't really have a name,' chuckles down-to-earth Rebecca, who has lived in the church-owned building since 2008. Her father is a minister at the church next door and before she, her three children (Lucas, 20, Ester, 13 and Elias, 10) and her husband Bruno moved in, the lofty flat was previously home to Rebecca's aunt and uncle. 'I remember visiting this apartment when I was a teenager,' she recalls. 'Perhaps other people way back in my family have lived here, too. It's a nice thought.'

Spending time in Rebecca's home is inspiring and endlessly fascinating. Unusual finds from Vietnam sit alongside her own designer creations and carefully selected vintage pieces, creating an effortlessly chic interior that's filled with dramatic contrasts.

There are painted white wooden floorboards and rough, raw cement walls. Her desk is sleek, new, white and glossy, but the handmade basket beneath it is rustic, artisanal and ancient. She expertly combines the hand-crafted and organic with clean, modern lines.

'If everything looks old and trashy, it becomes too trashy,' explains Rebecca. 'I think it's important to have something very defined and square up against the roughness. I like to mix old and new together. Contrasts make life interesting and exciting – in interiors, with people, in many areas.'

Having studied ceramics and glass at design school, Rebecca graduated in 1999 and teamed up with fellow student friends to form a creative design studio. 'It was fantastic and we did a lot of work for exhibitions,' she recalls. 'We just wanted to make art. We didn't care about the business side of things, but we couldn't live from it, of course.'

When Rebecca's youngest child was just four months old, she and husband Bruno decided to leave Denmark. They upped sticks and moved their family to Vietnam. Travelling up to the mountains where tribal people lived

BELOW Designer, vintage and handmade pieces share the same space, with dramatic results. Here, an Arne Jacobsen floor lamp and a modern sofa sit alongside an antique rug and a printed throw from Vietnam. The metal basket is one of Rebecca's own designs for Ro.

RIGHT The Sheba statue proudly on display in Rebecca's hallway is from central Vietnam. 'Often the tribes have roots back to Cambodia or Burma. The ancient statues remain long after the people have gone,' explains Rebecca. 'She looks so friendly and benign.'

offered Rebecca endless inspiration and she returned with many treasures. 'When an object has been used by someone, it has a tactility, evidence of time passing and traces of use,' reveals Rebecca. 'I have a tribal headpiece, which I bought from a woman and it's particularly precious to me because of the memories attached to it.'

While in Vietnam, Rebecca built up a design brand from scratch with a partner and then, on her return to Copenhagen in 2008, she joined Georg Jensen as a product developer working on Christmas products. By the time she left in 2013, she was Design Director.

'I was working with lots of steel objects at Georg Jensen,' says Rebecca. 'I have a

ceramics background, so working with shiny, steel pieces all the time didn't feel quite right. I wanted to work with other materials.'

And so, Ro Collection was born. 'The name Ro is about being quiet and grounded. I work with hand-picked designers who are at a stage in their lives where they're not just motivated by money – they want to make a durable product using crafted materials.'

For her shop, Rebecca seeks out artistic makers who have 'the Ro factor'. 'When I look at a designer, I don't care how many products they have made for well-known brands. I don't find that very interesting. What matters to me is the person behind the objects and the way

they work. It's about making things in materials that look beautiful, durable and sustainable. I want products that aren't "screamy" or so loud that you tire of them. It would be nice if the objects I sell are considered future classics.'

Her online realm is minimalistic but not pretentious, and the virtual shelves are lined with pared-back yet stunning designs. Rebecca's Japanesque ceramic bowls and intricate copper-mesh baskets sit comfortably next to sculptural wooden pebbles by Rune Frederiksen and delicate glass vases by Nina Erichsen. Throughout the site, the styled images are interspersed with sketches and diagrams, revealing the design processes behind the products.

ABOVE Rebecca has perfected the art of contrast and balance in her home, creating expertly edited spaces that are chic but never too cool to be welcoming. For example, her glossy, contemporary desk (with a sleek iMac computer) is offset beautifully with a vintage mid-century chair and rustic, tribal accessories from Vietnam. Here, less is more. Every single thing of beauty can be appreciated and nothing is superfluous.

'Often, I'm divided between the very organic and things that are really straight and square. I try to achieve a balance between the two.'

Rebecca explains: 'I want to emphasize the art behind the designs, to share thoughts and drawings and go back to core values. Some designers work only on computers, but my focus is on the art process, which often starts with hand-drawing.'

This intrinsic love of art is evident in Rebecca's own home, where oil paintings, antiques, tribal finds and music (Rebecca is a keen pianist) merge to create a warm, welcoming, culture-rich realm. It's beguiling – but never staged. This is a family home, full of hustle and bustle. Friends sip wine in the kitchen, her kids play computer games in the 'snug' and Kitty the cheeky cat ensures nothing remains pristine for too long.

Rebecca relishes new challenges and has enjoyed setting up Ro, but despite her obvious glee for her new-found independence, she admits

LEFT The dark blue colour in the 'snug' creates an intimate feeling. 'Using a dark wall colour in a small room makes it cosy,' explains Rebecca. 'This is where I listen to music or read a book. I used the same calming colour for the Ro logo.'
OPPOSITE FROM TOP LEFT In the hallway, a bright coat stand from Hay makes a statement; the wooden bowl was designed for Georg Jensen – 'It's like a rounded triangle; 'the shape is inspired by Japanese pottery and I've used a similar shape for my ceramic bowls at Ro. I'm crazy about it!' observes Rebecca; this plaster prototype will soon become a teapot for Ro.

running a small business is not without its difficulties. 'It's expensive to produce your own work,' she says, frankly. 'Production is also a challenge. Achieving the right quality and not being cheated by your suppliers is a huge challenge.' While Rebecca finds the press and public relations side of the venture easy, the sales aspect is more of a chore for the humble designer. 'Facing the market is very difficult for a person like me. I'm not just selling a toothbrush or something. I'm selling my own work that I have put my heart, my emotions and

everything into. It's like offering yourself. So, if somebody were to say they don't like my work, it would feel personal.'

Rebecca's philosophy for her online brand is clear. 'Ro is a contrast to the superficial, the transient, the fastness and the perishable in our time.' Her designs, and those she chooses, all have thoughtful narratives behind them. 'Within this passion lies the key to real sustainability,' explains Rebecca. A charming pioneer with a clear vision and a back-to-basics approach, the Ro revolution is in safe hands.

REBECCA LOVES:
- Aarstiderne: www.aarstiderne.com
- Cinnober: www.cinnobershop.dk
- Spark Design Space: www.sparkdesignspace.com

TOP E-TAILING TIPS:
- Make sure your online shop is easy to navigate. Learn user behaviours.

- Keep the design of your site simple – don't confuse your customers.

- Ensure security is your priority. Use a well-known payment platform.

- Be honest at all times. If a product is not available, make that clear.

MAKERS

Highly skilled artisanal sellers who
craft their products by hand

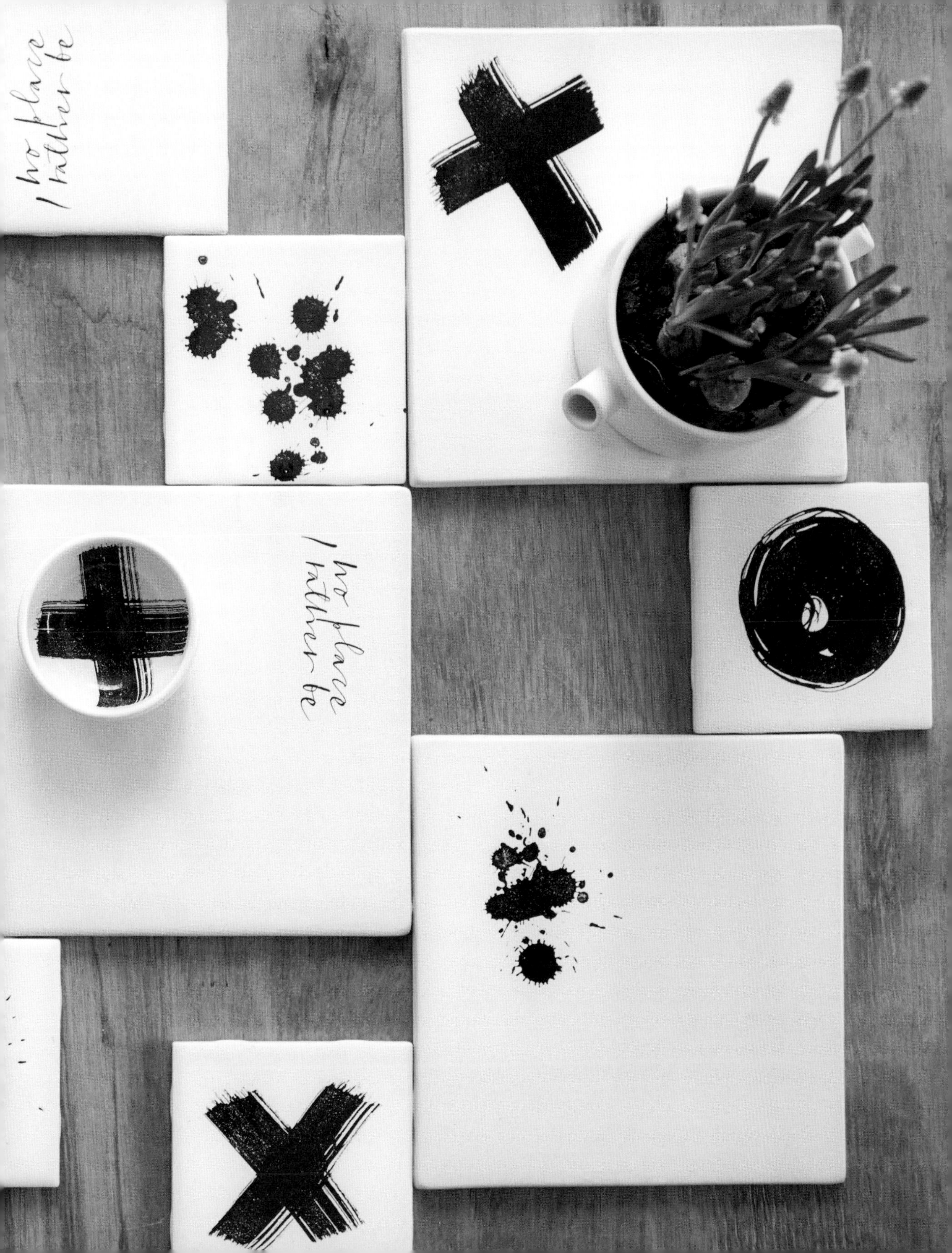
no place
I rather be
no place
I rather be

YLVA SKARP

www.ylvaskarp.se

Swedish calligrapher and designer Ylva Skarp lives with her husband
Daniel and their children Hugo (16) and Vega (13) in a converted
lakeside schoolhouse set in a picturesque corner of rural Sweden.
From her studio, she designs her own range of signature-style home
accessories, featuring cutting-edge lettering designs. It's calligraphy,
yes, but not as you know it…

**FACT FILE /
YLVA SHARP**

CHIC BOUTIQUER
Ylva Skarp
BASED
Leksand, Sweden
ONLINE SHOP
Ylva Skarp
ADDRESS
www.ylvaskarp.se
LAUNCHED
2010
STOCK
Graphic home accessories
such as art prints, cushion
covers and ceramic tiles,
featuring calligraphy lettering
SHOP STYLE
Industrial, graphic,
monochrome
HOME
A renovated former school-
house overlooking a lake in
Leksand, central Sweden

Ylva Skarp has always loved lettering, but it wasn't until she saw a television interview with a calligrapher who did the lettering for the Nobel Prize certificate that she realized it could become a career. 'When I was growing up, I didn't know that being creative could be more than a hobby,' she explains. Inspired, Ylva decided to move to London and study calligraphy at the Roehampton Institute. She returned to Sweden in 1995 and started her own business in Stockholm.

'At the beginning, as most calligraphers do, I did commission work,' remembers Ylva. 'I worked on invitations, logos and certificates, but I didn't want that to be the whole business. I always wanted to do my own thing and put together my own range of products.'

When Ylva moved back to her childhood home town of Leksand in 2003, she opened up a small summer shop in the garden. 'My first designs were hand-painted phrases on elegant, wooden boards,' she recalls. 'People could commission their own personalized messages, but after a while I decided to branch out in a different way.'

The popularity of her work meant she couldn't keep up with demand. 'You get to a point where you can't do everything by hand yourself,' she

PREVIOUS PAGES Evidence of Ylva's creative skills are everywhere in her stylish home, from her hand-painted dining table ('made from four old school desks') to her clever tile-effect kitchen wall, which is actually just painted black lines.
THIS PAGE Ylva made the coffee tables from plywood and castors. 'The industrial lights were already here when we bought the house, in an outbuilding that used to be a tin workshop and is now my studio.'

RIGHT The contrast of black and white in the Scandinavian-style kitchen provides a simple canvas to display things on. 'Painting a wall is a quick and easy way to update your look,' advises Ylva.

FAR RIGHT A stunning reclaimed stove provides a cosy corner in Ylva's sleek, monochrome kitchen. 'You can cook on it,' explains Ylva. 'We use it at Christmas and it creates a really festive atmosphere.'

explains. 'Doing commissions was taking up a lot of my time and it just wasn't that much fun – I was doing the same things, like birth certificates, over and over again. I wanted to focus on my own work instead.' Entrepreneurial Ylva decided to start producing her own products on a larger scale and began having her artistic script-like designs printed onto ceramics and cushions, too.

She launched her web shop in 2010 and, thanks to a huge Instagram following and a loyal online fan base, her work has achieved cult-like status among those in the know and her collection goes from strength to strength. Her home accessories are adorned with uplifting slogans in her trademark hand lettering: 'Remind yourself of who you are'; 'If you never try, you never know'.

Ylva is thrilled by the success of her company, but now faces new challenges. 'I want to get back to being creative again,' she says, wistfully. 'I need somebody to run the business, so I can return to the studio. I'm really fortunate to be able to do this for a living, though. I'm blessed.'

OPPOSITE BOTTOM The enormous open-plan living room is subtly divided into various zones, with a raised TV area, separated from the rest of the space by a panel of glass windows that lets light through.

THIS PAGE The 1950s chair was already in the building when Ylva and her family moved in. 'We salvaged the old tin soldier museum sign when we renovated the building,' says Ylva, who has enjoyed preserving the building's history.

STYLE TIP
If you opt for raw concrete elements, ensure you soften the look with fluffy rugs, natural materials and painted areas so that your room feels warm.

The home Ylva shares with husband Daniel and their two children provides the perfect space to showcase her beautiful products. A former school, the building was being used as a tin soldier museum when they bought it. Requiring a lot of renovation, Ylva admits that initally the unusual house was a daunting project. 'I found it really hard to make it homely because it was so spacious, with high ceilings,' she explains. 'It was a bit overwhelming at first, but over time we've realized what works. I really like minimalistic style, but it doesn't work in this house – it needs a bit more texture to feel like a home. Otherwise it's sterile and cold.'

Walls are painted white, grey and black, but with raw wooden beams, concrete panels and rustic, whitewashed boards, the interior of the house features a plethora of different finishes and textures that combine to create a layered, warm look.

The lofty former school hall posed a problem – Ylva wanted to keep the impressive sense of space and height, while zoning the room into more functional family areas. Cleverly, she and Daniel decided to install a raised platform, separated from the rest of the hall by a glass-window room divider and accessed via stairs, to create a cosy TV den. The overall impact of the huge space is not diminished, but the room is now split into two useable living areas, which feel warm and welcoming, despite the airy proportions.

OPPOSITE Floor-to-ceiling shelves laden with books surround the striking doorway in the living room. 'The huge doors were boxed into the walls when we moved in, so we didn't know they were there until we started to renovate,' says Ylva. **ABOVE FROM LEFT** Ylva's pared-back calligraphy creations are on display throughout her home. 'The leather chair is another vintage piece that was here when we moved in,' recalls Ylva; upstairs, her daughter's stylish bedroom has a fun chalkboard feature wall.

ABOVE The master bedroom overlooks the lake and is awash with light, thanks to a vast window that stretches the width of the room. Textured, retro wallpaper and a tall headboard give this space an air of understated elegance. **OPPOSITE FROM TOP LEFT** School gymnastic exercise prints found in the loft during the renovation now take pride of place – 'I do the exercises every day!' jokes Ylva; a minimalistic, modern pendant light illuminates the hallway; Ylva has filled her home with playful touches – here, two small plastic animals create a quirky vignette.

Thanks to the previous incarnations the quirky building has had, it contained many treasures that Ylva and Daniel were delighted to discover, such as stunning mid-century chairs, old school tables, industrial-style workshop lamps and even a series of instructional gymnastics exercise prints found in the attic. Now, these incredible posters are displayed on a wall in the hallway, while a sign from the building's museum days is propped up in the dining room. 'We knew this building had great potential, but we uncovered some unexpected finds during renovation,' reveals Ylva, happily. A pair of huge wooden doors, for example, had been boxed into the hall walls and are now reinstated in their original frame.

As well as having bags of character and charm, the generously sized home enjoys an enviable location, too, on the banks of the vast Siljan lake. Ylva and her family eat meals of fresh, deep pink wild salmon when it's in season, go ice-skating in the winter and sunbathe on the deck of their boat house in the summer. 'It's a good life,' agrees Ylva. 'I loved the hustle and bustle of Stockholm, but returning to Leksand has been great for the kids.'

Whether she's redecorating her home or working on a new design for her brand, Ylva pours her infectious energy into everything she does. 'My name means she-wolf in Swedish,' she chuckles. 'So, watch out!'

YLVA LOVES:
- Rum 21: www.rum21.se
- Organic Makers: www.organicmakers.se
- Granit: www.granit.com

TOP E-TAILING TIPS:
- Unfortunately, it's not enough to have good products. You have to present them in a really good way and your site has to look professional all the way through.

- It's important to be able to edit your website yourself so that you can manage it whenever you want.

- I always put a handwritten thank-you note in with packages. Even though my business is growing bigger, it's important to me that things still feel personal.

- There is such competition that you really need to find your own path and your own expression. It's how you can stand out from the crowd.

THIS PAGE Maryanne and Aaron found their beautiful sideboard in a vintage furniture store in New York. 'We've filled it with our record collection,' says Maryanne. 'We were thinking about getting a TV to go on top, but we never got around to it.'
OPPOSITE The vintage Moroccan rug is from Etsy. 'I like to support sustainable, small businesses,' explains Maryanne. 'The feeling I get when I go in a big department store just doesn't feel like love.'

MARYANNE MOODIE

www.maryannemoodie.com

Australian textile artist Maryanne Moodie weaves contemporary wall hangings from a studio in the Brooklyn brownstone apartment she shares with husband Aaron and their son Murray. Her cutting-edge colour combinations and the thriving online community she has created set Maryanne apart from the crowd.

FACT FILE /
MARYANNE MOODIE

CHIC BOUTIQUER
Maryanne Moodie
BASED
New York, USA
ONLINE SHOP
Maryanne Moodie
ADDRESS
www.maryannemoodie.com
or www.etsy.com/uk/shop/
MaryanneMoodie
LAUNCHED
2013
STOCK
Weaving kits and yarn packs,
bespoke woven wall hangings
SHOP STYLE
Contemporary, sustainable,
handmade
HOME
The top-floor apartment
in a terraced Brooklyn
brownstone house, with
tin ceiling tiles, a 1940s
kitchen and elegant
fireplaces

LEFT A modern geometric side table sits alongside crafty creations and vintage finds in the living room. The walls are adorned with Maryanne's colourful weavings and various pieces of art from swaps Maryanne has done with other makers. 'One talented artist painted a bespoke canvas for me, featuring elements from my home, which she had only seen on my Instagram feed,' she says. 'It's really lovely.' OPPOSITE Maryanne collects vintage woven wall hangings from the 1960s and 1970s. 'Objects feel richer when they have a history – I like to know that they have had a life before and I'm comforted to think that they will be owned and loved by somebody else when I pass them along. I won't own them forever. Their journey will continue.'

Maryanne Moodie's fashion-forward woven wall hangings are popular all over the globe and bloggers, pinners and crafters go wild for her striking yarn creations. The weaving revival might be in full swing, but Maryanne is always one step ahead of the trends.

'I grew up in Melbourne, Australia, with five siblings,' she says. 'Some people had really creative childhoods that sound enchanted and delightful, but my mum was just getting through it all. She was so busy cooking and cleaning that crafting wasn't a priority.'

Maryanne's creativity flourished during her teenage years when she and her sister would scour the local 'op' (charity/thrift) shops for bargain buys. 'I loved the hunt,' she recalls. 'I'd spend ages looking at the sparkles, the clothes and the vintage textiles. I learned early on that I love fashion, fabrics and tactile things.'

A deep appreciation of hand-crafted work was instilled in Maryanne at this stage, when she started to notice that items produced before the 1970s were carefully made and cared for. 'You could trace the history of a garment by studying it,' she explains. 'Sometimes, a button would have been replaced, a hemline lowered or a dart moved – you could follow the life story.'

Her love of all things vintage meant that by the time Maryanne was in her twenties, she was working as a primary school teacher in the day and running an online

vintage emporium in her spare time, specializing in second-hand clothes and selling via Facebook to legions of followers. But she craved a more creative pursuit.

'The crunch time for me came when I couldn't remember what I'd bought my sister for her birthday the year before and, when I asked her, she couldn't remember either!' chuckles Maryanne. 'I thought: this is horrible. I just go into a shop and pick something up and it doesn't mean anything to her or to me.' After that she began to craft her own presents for friends and family.

It wasn't until three and a half years ago, when she was pregnant with her son Murray, that Maryanne had

a chance encounter that would change the course of her life. 'I was helping to pack up the art store room at the school I taught in and I stumbled across a vintage wooden loom. It was going to be thrown out, so I took it home and had a go. Aaron, my partner, had got a job in New York and was able to support me, so the pressure was off a bit and I had time to experiment.'

She didn't have any yarn, so used fluorescent string and jute at first and wove small coasters just for fun. 'I shared them with my friends online,' says Maryanne with a smile. 'Before long, people were asking if they were for sale. The more I made, the more people wanted them.'

ABOVE FROM LEFT The kitchen is filled with handmade mugs and rustic, wooden utensils; Maryanne says the apartment's kitchen was 'a clincher', thanks to the original period details. 'The farmhouse sink, the soap nooks – we just knew it was the home for us!' Trailing plants dangle from shelves and climb around the windows. 'It's really important to me to have living plants at home,' reveals Maryanne.

Despite this interest, Maryanne resisted the urge to rush into selling online. 'Aaron gave me some good advice. He said: "You're learning something new. Don't sell anything until it is the best possible product it can be. You need to sort out your materials and process, and make sure they are really perfect." He was right.'

Maryanne took her time and honed her skills, practising techniques and exploring ideas. Online exposure before the launch of her shop meant that people were talking about Maryanne's work long before it was available. 'I didn't sell anything for a year,' she reveals. 'I was just sharing my work online and giving a few wall hangings away to friends. One hung it in her fashion boutique. Another put one on the wall of her café. Then, blogger Lucy Feagins from The Design Files spotted me on Instagram and posted about my weaving and I was amazed at the response.'

By the time she set up her Etsy shop, Maryanne's work was in hot demand. These days, she focuses on commissions, sells kits and runs sought-after workshops. She weaves every day in her airy top-floor studio in the rented home she, Aaron and Murray moved to in New York.

'People told us we needed a lift/elevator, a door man and a ground-floor flat because we had a toddler, but after seeing a few soulless, cramped apartments, we decided we wanted the top floor of a brownstone, with light, air and space,' explains Maryanne. 'We love older-style properties, so were lucky to find an apartment with lots of pretty original features that's close to a beautiful park.'

Tin ceiling tiles, exposed brick walls, marble fire surrounds, window shutters – Maryanne and Aaron's home oozes character and charm.

'Don't sell anything until it is the best possible product it can be… sort out your materials and process; make sure they are perfect.'

BELOW The rocking chair was a gift from Maryanne's friends when she was pregnant with Murray. 'We didn't want any "baby" things. It was a great breast-feeding chair and much better looking than those ugly padded nursing models, plus it's got longevity, too,' she says.

FAR LEFT The master bedroom is filled with weavings and quirky creations made by fellow artists. Small potted plants are scattered here and there. 'Plants cost the same as flowers,' reasons Maryanne. 'Even if they just last six months or a year, then that's still better value than a bunch of flowers.' **LEFT** Thanks to contemporary artworks, green plants and impressive period features, the couple's home has a laid-back, bohemian vibe.

Moving from Australia to the US meant shipping their possessions, which was a challenge. 'Our furniture didn't arrive for four months and we just had an air mattress,' remembers Maryanne. 'I think it's really important to feel at home, so I bought lovely bed linen, towels and plants.' Their home is fully furnished now and an incredibly inspiring space, where homemade woven wall hangings, vintage finds and pieces of art by fellow Etsy sellers create a heady mix of colours and a cosy, homely feel.

Maryanne's studio contains several looms of different sizes and a huge selection of yarns, arranged by colour. 'Most of my yarn cones are from former textile factories. New yarn is very formal and it all looks the same. When you use vintage yarn, there are little faults. You can never recreate the same piece twice because once the yarn's gone, it's gone,' she explains.

Like many creative activities, Maryanne says weaving is 'meditative', and she enjoys 'just going with the flow'. 'My favourite pieces are definitely the more organic ones when I get to feel the yarns and make decisions as I go along, allowing the piece to naturally move through the process. I prefer weaving those to the very strict geometric designs, which involve exactness.'

Interacting offline with her online community is important to Maryanne, both from a business perspective and a personal one. 'In Melbourne, I once put a huge loom in the window of a florist's shop and chose yarns that matched the colours of the seasonal flowers. I sat in the window for a week and lots of people popped in to have a go.' Passersby and online followers alike spent time with Maryanne, weaving, chatting and learning, while helping to create a community wall hanging. Now, it's her Brooklyn workshops that give Maryanne the most joy. 'I love being in a room of excited, interested people – mostly women. The atmosphere is a bit like a women's circle, with people of all ages and backgrounds learning skills together and chatting. It harks back to a time when grandmothers, aunts, mothers and girls would sit together and craft.'

So, what does the future hold for this talented weaver, who expertly weaves together not only yarns but stories and the threads of communities? 'I want to push my practice by collaborating with other people who want to push their boundaries a bit,' says Maryanne. 'I'm planning to work with an industrial designer, who can create 3D shapes for me to weave.' Watch this space.

THIS PAGE Maryanne's display cases are the result of another art swap with a glass artist who runs a shop called Glass and Snacks. 'She also made the waning and waxing moon garland above my bed,' says Maryanne. 'We'd been following one another online for a time and we arranged to make each other something.'

THIS PAGE The wall-hung shelves are from IKEA and Aaron sprayed the brackets yellow. The storage unit was custom-made for Maryanne. 'The way I work is fluid and free,' she explains. 'I have to see everything at once, so I can pull a yarn out and hold it against others.'
OPPOSITE FROM TOP LEFT Maryanne's home studio is filled with colourful yarns and assorted looms.

MARYANNE LOVES:
- Brooklyn Flea Market: www.brooklynflea.com
- ABC Carpet and Home: www.abchome.com
- Etsy: www.etsy.com

TOP E-TAILING TIPS:
- Don't sell the first thing that you make. Wait for a while and hone your skills until your work is of top quality and you can charge the right price.

- Let your customers see the real you. The behind-the-scenes posts where I share my process always get the most likes.

- Success is partly about having an awareness, noticing, listening and going with your gut instinct. If you have a three- or five-year plan, it can take away from opportunities that present themselves along the way.

- Create a community around what you do. It's important to work out what your story is and how people can relate to you.

STUDIO JOO

www.studiojoo.com

Multi-talented ceramicist Elaine Tian lives in a 1940s apartment block in the Ditmas Park area of Brooklyn with her partner Baxter Holland. When she's not throwing delicate porcelain creations on her pottery wheel, Elaine is busy making her own bespoke lighting, sculpting bowls from paper, sketching or hula-hooping. Few people are as gifted in so many diverse artistic areas, but Elaine's focus is on her celebrated ceramic work, which she sells online.

Elaine has an interesting history. Born in Singapore but brought up in Sydney, Australia, in the 1990s, she studied sculpture and then did a masters degree in design studies. She came to New York in 2001 and considers it home.

Elaine spent the first part of her career happily working as a graphic designer for magazines and private clients, designing everything from page layouts to logos. It wasn't until 2012 that she fell in love with porcelain. 'I took a pottery wheel class and just got completely addicted,' she remembers. 'Having a degree in sculpture gave me an advantage because I was already familiar with the materials, but I'd never used a pottery wheel before. I was instantly smitten.'

There followed a tricky transition period, when Elaine was still working as a freelance designer but was also trying to spend as much time as possible in the ceramics studio. Some days she would have a meeting with a client and on others she'd be caked in clay dust. 'My addiction got so bad that I started giving my freelance jobs away so I could spend more and more time on my ceramics. Now, Studio Joo is my focus and I can just be myself without having to juggle so many things.'

Elaine's delicate creations are all one-offs – elegant, sculptural porcelain bowls and vases, with watery, fluid glazes. It's exquisite, but she modestly refrains from referring to herself as a potter. 'I'm a designer who works with clay,' she says. 'There are potters who have trained

ABOVE With a plush rug, sleek furniture and touches of brass, the living room is glamorous with an Art Deco flavour. Elaine's enormous sofa is vintage. 'I found it in a shop called White Trash in the East Village, New York,' she reveals. 'It had been reupholstered for a movie set, so it's in perfect condition.' The fabric on the sofa is from Tokyo. Elaine made the orange geometric cushions using a pair of vintage 1960s curtains she bought in the Netherlands. The large pink artwork above the sofa is an eBay find.

FACT FILE / STUDIO JOO

CHIC BOUTIQUER
Elaine Tian

BASED
New York, USA

ONLINE SHOP
Studio Joo

ADDRESS
www.studiojoo.com

LAUNCHED
2012

STOCK
Hand-thrown porcelain-ware

SHOP STYLE
Considered, artistic, elegant

HOME
A Brooklyn apartment in
a 1940s building, with high
ceilings and period features

THIS PAGE The unit in the hallway is an IKEA cabinet that came with metal doors, but creative Elaine replaced them with wood for a bespoke look. 'I bought some cheap pine boards for about six dollars each and stained them,' she reveals. The iconic Hans Wegner chair was bought on eBay.

LEFT One of Elaine's handmade floor lamps makes an impact in the living room. 'I think of my home in terms of vignettes,' admits Elaine. 'Coming from the magazine world, I'm very aware of how my home looks. I'm always composing, always curating.'
BELOW The living room has a gallery-like quality, with interesting artworks and objects displayed carefully against white walls. 'Baxter is serious about vinyl,' laughs Elaine. 'I have a bunch, too. We both like the vintage sound quality, but we appreciate the cover designs, too.'

as apprentices under master potters for years and years, so I still don't consider myself a proper potter really, although I use the same tools and share similar processes.'

Porcelain completely changed Elaine's practice. 'I was using dark clay, but when I discovered porcelain everything fell into place,' she says. 'The focus of my work has always been mark-making and alteration. With porcelain, I felt as though I could work the material like paper. I've done a lot of sculpture with paper and folding, building processes. With porcelain, everything just made sense. The whiteness of it was the perfect canvas – I've stuck with it ever since.'

Part of the appeal of ceramics to Elaine is that it's so different from her past graphic design work. 'When you're a graphic designer, everything is precision-heavy – you're pursuing perfection,' she explains. 'You check and double-check, there are edits and it's a whole cycle of checks before something gets published. There's no room for error. If you make a mistake in a magazine or on a logo, it gets reproduced many times. There's no appreciation of the imperfect.'

Nowadays, rather than working with grids and minutiae, she feels more free and loves to embrace the essence of the Japanese aesthetic: *wabi-sabi* (侘寂), the art of imperfection. 'I can be technically proficient, but can also appreciate the humble, human qualities of what I make. You can see my fingerprints and where I didn't sand the glaze perfectly, but the imperfections are appreciated – they show that somebody made it. It's the opposite of mass production. Every piece is a one-off.'

Elaine's home is elegant and the perfect setting for her stunning creations. Baxter and Elaine were instantly drawn to the generous proportions of the rooms in their apartment, the high ceilings and the spacious, open-plan layout, which provides space to work in as well as live.

'I love the solidity of this building,' says Elaine. 'It was built during the war years, so there's a bomb shelter in the basement, which is now used as a bike storage room.'

Carefully selected vintage furniture is combined with handmade elements that Elaine has created herself, iconic designer classics and eclectic artwork gathered over the years. The result is a serene space – where nothing unnecessary distracts from the beauty of the objects within it.

'You can see my fingerprints and where I didn't sand the glaze perfectly, but the imperfections are appreciated – they show that somebody made it.'

STYLE TIP
In a dark corner,
lean a large floor-
standing mirror against
the wall to reflect light
and give the illusion
of a bigger space.

THIS PAGE & OPPOSITE Calm and
orderly, the bedroom is a restful,
elegant space. Framed photos of
Elaine's mother, taken by her father,
hang in a corner. 'My father was
a keen photographer,' she explains.
'He was a huge influence on me.
He worked as an art director in
the advertising industry and took
amazing photos of my mum.' The
kilim rug is from Egypt and was
bought online. The sideboard is
by Maine and the blue chair is
from Blu Dot.

LEFT The kitchen is tidy and organized. It's easy for an apartment to get cluttered,' admits Elaine. 'We're constantly editing, but there's a balance between an uncluttered, curated space and a home that's welcoming. I don't want my home to look like a set from *Mad Men* or a catalogue – I like handmade things and drawings by friends.'

OPPOSITE FROM TOP The light fitting above the dining table is from Design Within Reach; Elaine's bamboo matcha whisk is called a 'chasen', and the stand that the whisk sits on is called a 'kusenaoshi' – 'I know a lot about tea ceremonies because one of my clients was a big tea company,' explains Elaine; sometimes customers commission multiples of the same bowl, but Elaine's pieces are all unique. 'There are so many variables, from where you place a pot to how humid it is that day. To me, that's *wabi-sabi*.'

This is a creative home, with rich cultural material at every turn, interesting artifacts and quirky details. Stacks of design books sit alongside an impressive vinyl collection and all around there are fascinating pieces of art to admire. The highlights of the space are undoubtedly the striking light fixtures that she makes herself. Unphased by electrical wiring, Elaine has created show-stopping lights that give her home instant glamour.

'I struggle to find lights I like that I can afford,' says Elaine. 'I want well-made, beautiful things, but as lights are so expensive, it's sometimes easier just to make my own!' Unsurprisingly, like her porcelain, her lighting is highly sought after.

Ceramic design forces Elaine to engage mindfully with the present. 'You have to have a certain amount of concentration and control when you're throwing. It takes strength,' she explains. 'Clay forces you to be centred because you're focused on keeping your pot on the wheel and you're essentially defying gravity – pulling up the walls.' Her passion for pottery is infectious. 'I'm sure I sound like a hippy, but it's very human to work with earth,' she concludes. 'I just love it.'

ELAINE LOVES:
• Totokaelo: www.totokaelo.com
• 1stdibs: www.1stdibs.com
• Paddle8: www.paddle8.com

TOP E-TAILING TIPS:
• Good photography is essential. Learn a few tricks; invest in some basic equipment and some good photo-editing software. If you need guidance, hire a professional to help you. It makes such a difference.

• Wrap your products carefully. Couriers aren't always careful. My porcelain is fragile, so I double-box everything and use loads of packaging materials.

• Spend some time choosing the right platform for you. I use Big Cartel because it has subtle branding and lets me control the look and feel of my site.

• Organize your time. I spend a day a week doing non-studio work: admin, photo shoots, meetings, shipping, website updates, etc. Then I can be in the studio for the remaining days.

CURATORS

Stylish online shopkeepers who carefully curate ever-evolving collections

THIS PAGE The spacious oak extension designed by James houses the living room and has superb views of the sea, thanks to floor-to-ceiling windows facing the beach. The 'FIRE' sign was found in a local junk shop.

OPPOSITE A Welsh blanket door curtain hangs on a wooden tiller from a sailing boat. Vintage cinema seats and wood engravings by Gertrude Hermes (from the 1939 Penguin edition of *The Compleat Angler*) add subtle decoration.

FFOREST GENERAL STORES

www.fforest.bigcartel.com

Among the lobster pots and pebbles of picturesque Aberporth bay, on the Ceredigion coast in Wales, is a pretty, stone cottage, just a few metres from the beach. Sian Tucker and her partner James Lynch live here with their four sons, running fforest – a camp where they combine ethically sourced materials and local craft to create relaxed, comfortable and inspiring spaces where holidaymakers can stay and play. They have a café and a 'pizza tipi' as well as an online shop, with the outdoors at the core of all they do.

FACT FILE / FFOREST GENERAL STORES

CHIC BOUTIQUERS
Sian Tucker and
James Lynch
BASED
Cardigan, Wales
ONLINE SHOP
fforest general stores
ADDRESS
www.fforest.bigcartel.com
LAUNCHED
2010
STOCK
Welsh blankets, bushcraft
and camping kit, local
artisanal treats
SHOP STYLE
Warm, crafted comfort
HOME
An ancient fisherman's
cottage in Aberporth
harbour in Wales, with
stone walls, slate floors
and wooden beams

BELOW 'My four sons each gave me a cactus for my birthday,' says Sian. The kayak above was made in Wales. RIGHT A vintage enamel light hangs above the chunky kitchen island, which is topped with railway sleepers/railroad ties.

By the time they left London in 2005 to set up fforest in rural north Pembrokeshire, Sian and James felt they needed a change from city living. With four young boys, the call of the wild could no longer be ignored.

Both art school graduates (James studied graphics and Sian textile design), the couple had spent many happy years in Shoreditch, East London, where they worked as designers. They bought a furniture warehouse, rented out studio space to fellow creatives and lived in a romantic roof-top apartment, but over time, the area began to become less bohemian. The family upped sticks and moved to 'the wild west coast' of Wales. They bought fforest, a 200-acre farm on the edge of the beautiful River Teifi gorge, and created a camp – 'a kind of hotel made of canvas'. With geodesic domes and Scandinavian tipis, their dream was to: 'combine the life-enhancing feeling of living outdoors with simple comforts, all wrapped up in a magical setting'.

'We bought our home as a holiday cottage originally, 18 years ago,' explains Sian. 'It wasn't until much later in 2005 that we moved in full time. When the cottage next door became available a few years after that, we bought it and knocked a wall through to turn them into one big home,' she adds. Now, the living room, kitchen, master bedroom and bathroom are in one half, where Sian and James sleep, and the other house is entirely given over to their sons, with a relaxed TV den, bedrooms and bathroom – it's a teenagers' paradise.

'Old fishermen's cottages were built the wrong way around,' explains Sian. 'They were positioned end on to the sea, to protect them from wind and rain, but it means you can never appreciate the sea view!'

With this in mind, talented James designed an airy, contemporary extension – an enormous living/dining room made entirely from green oak, with vertical glass panels either side of the slate chimney breast in order that the stunning seascapes can be fully enjoyed. High, horizontal windows give the reassuring feeling that the house is completely enveloped by nature and almost part of the landscape itself. Ivy tendrils creep in through the frames.

'We love natural textures and materials,' says Sian. 'The original exterior walls of the cottage are exposed so we can appreciate the beauty of the stonework and we've surrounded ourselves with simple but beautiful wood and slate.'

Sian jokes that James is 'the designer' and her role is to 'buy clutter'. Modesty prevails – this is a dream team with a shared creative vision; a yin and yang partnership that results in inspiring and incredibly beautiful interiors. Vintage treasures such as enamel kettles and chic chairs are teamed with Welsh woven blankets, beachcombing finds and reindeer-skin rugs. It's eclectic, elemental, simple – stylish. But above all, it's warm and welcoming. This is a family home, where clogs and wellies line the walls of the hallway, the kitchen is a hub of activity and Arrow the border collie lollops from room to room, relishing the fun of it all.

'In the winter, when I'm not sleeping, I spend most of my time in the kitchen,' says Sian. 'That's my hub. James spends a lot of time working in his shed at the bottom of the garden. But in the summer, we both live outside.'

BELOW In the kitchen, skilful James has topped two IKEA freestanding sideboard units with hefty pieces of reclaimed wood that were originally synagogue benches. 'We bought lots of pews and cabinets in one batch and we've used the wood on our stair treads, window ledges and shelves, too,' says Sian. 'It's beautifully polished – by Jewish bottoms!'

THIS PAGE Sian loves vintage
kitchenalia. 'Old things last,' she
says. 'They don't fall to bits like
mass-produced stuff often does.'
The walls of the kitchen are 60-cm
(2-ft) deep. 'It's cool in the summer
– and in the winter!' jokes Sian.

'Big brands buy in bulk and charge competitive prices,' explains Sian, 'So we decided to specialize and sell carefully selected products online instead.'

As part of their fforest empire, the couple opened a bricks-and-mortar shop in Cardigan selling outdoor clothing and kayaks, but soon became aware that they couldn't compete with bigger shops, price-wise. 'Big brands buy in bulk and charge competitive prices,' explains Sian, 'So, we decided to specialize and sell carefully selected products online instead.'

The online fforest 'general store' is filled with things the fforest family lives and works with themselves. Welsh honey – sourced a few miles away – rustic aprons, beautiful blankets (woven exclusively for fforest using a vintage pattern that Sian adapted) and camping paraphernalia such as lanterns, knives and fforest-designed 'forager socks'. It's a beguiling and expertly edited store, filled with well-made, utilitarian treats.

This philosophy and impressive attention to detail pervades everything at fforest. 'We only put wild flowers in our holiday accommodation that we've grown ourselves and picked. We make all our own jams, chutneys and granola. We have a vegetable garden that provides fresh salad and herbs. It's hard to keep up with the demand when we're in the summer season, but it's well worth all the effort,' reveals Sian.

These days, the business is a family affair – during the busy months, Sian and James employ all of their sons and many of their friends, too. 'Last summer, the four boys ran the pizza tipi

ABOVE 'We've always had an outdoor shower – even in London, when we had one on the roof,' recalls Sian. 'The stone wall is the original external wall. We clad the interior with slate and wood, so it feels indoor–outdoor and cave-like. We can get the whole family in.' A tiny ivy tendril boldly clings to the window frame.

OPPOSITE The horizontal bedroom window has been designed so that the couple can enjoy the stunning panoramic sea views outside. Tongue-and-groove cladding and wide oak floorboards create a simple, Shaker-style backdrop for Sian's colourful Welsh blankets and cushions. The grey cushion is a fforest design, woven in an old wool mill near the River Teifi.

STYLE TIP
For a casual, country look, avoid symmetrical bed accessories like cushions and throws. Instead, choose one pattern, then mix various colours.

LEFT James collects vintage paddles and boat parts, and incorporates them into the home – as a coat rail in the hallway and above doorways as curtain poles. The slate slabs and coir matting are beautiful, natural and practical.
OPPOSITE TOP 'I have a bit of a "thing" for spoons,' confesses Sian. 'I collect handmade, Welsh ones and have done ever since we first moved here. They have such character. In general, everything we have is like these spoons – slightly mismatched and imperfect.'
OPPOSITE BELOW A map of Shoreditch by British artist Adam Dant hangs on the living room wall and is a reminder of the couple's earlier life in fashionable East London.

for us, which was great,' says Sian, happily. With so many events, locations and strands to this ever-expanding world, it's hard work, but the rewards of coastal life are rich indeed. 'We love living here,' says Sian. 'At low tide, we go on shore-side foraging expeditions for mussels, cockles and razor clams. We eat crab and freshly caught mackerel in the summer. The boys can run wild. It's bliss.'

One of the prints that fforest stocks features Welsh words that are important to the family: *Cwtch, Hiraeth, Twymder, Teulu, Nos, Tywydd, Bwyd, Cariad*, which translate as: 'Cosy, Longing, Warmth, Family, Night, Weather, Dance, Food, My Love.' These small pleasures convey the essence of their way of life – simple living and being connected to the natural world brings enormous wealth that far outweighs financial or material gain.

TOP E-TAILING TIPS:
• Don't attempt to compete with huge brands – just do your own thing and keep it simple. To make it work, you've got to be different and sell something that people can't get anywhere else.

• Unless you're good at website design, use a template platform. We use Big Cartel, which is already set up with PayPal and every feature you need. It just makes life so easy.

• Social media is important to spread the word about your shop. Have a presence on all platforms, but focus on one or two.

• Invest time and energy in beautiful photography. Images for online don't need to be massively high resolution – we often take photos on our phones.

LIEFS VAN MAANTJE

www.liefsvanmaantje.nl

Janneke van Houtum's online and offline worlds merge into one, magical realm. Her colourful home is filled with fun details, as is her whimsical web shop Liefs van Maantje, which translates as: 'Love from Moon'. Her online site is covered with tiny glittering stars and the virtual aisles are lined with quirky illustrated prints, while her home is a cheerful wonderland, a dream-like retreat from reality.

FACT FILE / LEIFS VAN MAANTJE

CHIC BOUTIQUER
Janneke van Houtum

BASED
Eindhoven, Netherlands

ONLINE SHOP
Liefs van Maantje

ADDRESS
www.liefsvanmaantje.nl

LAUNCHED
2013

STOCK
Illustrated prints, stationery and paper goods

SHOP STYLE
Colourful, cute, crafty

HOME
A 1920s terraced townhouse in Eindhoven, with high ceilings and airy, open-plan living space

OPPOSITE Janneke's colourful accessories stand out against white walls and frame her pretty, vintage stove. THIS PAGE The trio of prints on the wall behind the sofa are by New Zealand artist Ellen Giggenbach and are available in Janneke's shop.

STYLE TIP
Hang a selection of plates on the wall in a group like Janneke has done so that you can admire your prettiest china pieces every day.

There are many different motivations for starting to sell online, but Janneke set up her online paper goods shop because she wanted a creative project to sink her teeth into, following a bout of illness. 'A few years ago, I had a little setback – a burn-out. I needed to find a new way to energize myself,' explains Janneke. 'Putting together the shop was like therapy for me really. I realized it was important for me to have a creative outlet and it was wonderful to have a positive project to focus on. Sometimes, it's good to step out of your comfort zone.'

As she recovered at home, Janneke spent her days building her website and scouring the globe for stock to sell. 'I emailed illustrators all around the world and, bit by bit, my health returned and so did my confidence. It was so fulfilling to do my own thing. I built the website over six months and launched it in late 2013.'

Liefs van Maantje allowed Janneke to indulge her life-long passion for illustration. 'I've always loved children's books,' she says. 'I work in a day-care centre and have two sons of my own now, too, so I'm able to enjoy kids' books every day! A lot of the products I sell are inspired by childhood.'

Janneke's collection is unique – her carefully selected paper decorations, stickers, greeting cards and posters are sourced from near and far. 'I deliberately include products by both well-known and lesser-known artists,'

she explains. 'I want an eclectic offering that nobody will find elsewhere.' The thrill of stumbling across a 'gem' always excites Janneke. 'I put a lot of time and effort into finding new names and I get a real kick out of discovering illustrators who are not so well known.'

The three-bedroom home she shares with husband Jeroen and their two sons Raave (6) and Midas (4) is an extension of her creative vision. Janneke enjoys playing with decorative details, treating the rooms as a canvas for telling stories.

Garlands of pompoms and paper decorations adorn the windows and living room walls; here, colour and pattern are embraced at every opportunity. This is a

home where fun reigns and the usual rules do not apply – magical, dream-like details can be found in every corner. Tiny bird stickers perch above the front door, green magnetic leaves turn radiator pipes into giant beanstalks and even the light switches have been given jolly, smiling faces.

Janneke particularly enjoyed decorating her sons' bedrooms, which are wonderlands filled with giant toadstools, a wooden tree, huge duck and goose lamps and garden gnomes. Stepping into Janneke's Eindhoven home is like walking into the pages of a children's storybook. It's refreshing to find a home that doesn't take itself too seriously.

'We moved here in 2012,' says Janneke. 'Before, we lived in a soulless 1980s flat in

ABOVE Janneke's home has elegant period features such as the traditional black and white floor tiles in the kitchen and hallway; the wall sticker is by artist Blanca Gómez and the way it's positioned invites you up the staircase. OPPOSITE The 1930s larder unit is a vintage Piet Zwart piece and was bought second hand online. Despite the fact that it was 'a dirty yellow colour and stained with tobacco smoke', Janneke loved the original glass and could see the potential for upcycling it.

THIS PAGE Janneke says that vinyl flooring is a practical choice for children's bedrooms. 'It looks great and it's easy to clean, too.' Tiny magnetic leaves turn a water pipe into a beanstalk. 'Decorating is the same as life – you have to work with what you've got and make the best of a situation,' chuckles Janneke.

RIGHT & FAR RIGHT The boys' bedrooms are imaginative and magical. The goose lamp is vintage, a hand-me-down from Janneke's mother, while the 1950s woodland-themed classroom posters were picked up at flea markets and found online. A snug space under the stairs provides a cosy bed nook for Raave.

the centre of the city, but I always wanted a 1920s house with panelled doors and plenty of character.' It was the airy open-plan ground floor that the couple instantly fell for. 'The dining area has a huge skylight, which floods the room with light and there's a nice garden, too, which is great for the kids.'

While the structure of the house didn't need major work, Jeroen and Janneke redecorated it from top to bottom, painting floorboards and walls. The staircase is painted in a striking jet black, while a wall in younger son Midas's room is a sunny, bold yellow.

'I love to shop online and sniff out vintage finds at flea markets,' reveals Janneke, who has a gift for spotting the unusual and beautiful. 'I found some mid-century woodland posters for my son's bedroom a while ago and I love the history they have. I like the idea that they've had a previous life – it gives them character.'

Other second-hand trophies include a stunning 1930s kitchen larder unit that Janneke has rejuvenated with a coat of pale blue paint and a roll of dainty bird-patterned vintage wallpaper, which she has used to paper an alcove in the master bedroom.

Part of the charm of Janneke's home is her skill for mixing handmade items with hand-me-downs and new buys, to create

ABOVE A bright yellow wall makes a big impact in Midas's bedroom, while toadstool decorations create a fantastical feel. 'We bought the small retro cupboard in a little local vintage store, which is one of those rare shops that's filled with beautiful things. The owners do their job with pleasure and love, and that makes shopping there special.'

LEFT Janneke says the attic bedroom is 'still a work in progress'. She loves the beams, which give the room height and an airy feel. 'They were dark wood when we first moved in, but we painted them white to freshen up the look,' she explains. OPPOSITE FROM TOP LEFT Janneke has fitted colourful mismatched knobs to the landing cupboards and drawers; the bedroom wallpaper is vintage and was bought in Sweet, in Belgium, and Janneke sewed the 1950s-style curtain beneath the basin herself, to conceal shoe storage; rolls of pretty, floral papers fill buckets, ready for wrapping up shop orders. The colourful rug is from Rice.

a cosy, welcoming feel that's layered and relaxed. 'My mother sews patchwork quilts and I inherited the corner cabinet in the dining room from my grandmother,' says Janneke. Many of the objects she surrounds herself with have personal meanings and are imbued with love.

Juggling a full-time job with bringing up two children and running an online business is tricky, but Janneke enjoys her various responsibilities and manages her time carefully. 'I run the web shop in the evenings and at weekends,' she explains. 'I wrap packages in the evenings and Jeroen drops them off at the post office in the mornings – we've got a good system in place! Maybe some day I will be able to make a full-time living from it, but for now I have to fit it around my other commitments. Working on the shop never feels like a chore because I love what I'm doing.'

JANNEKE LOVES:
- Nina Invorm: www.etsy.com/nl/shop/ninainvorm
- Petit Pan: www.petitpan.com
- Dreumes Dromen: www.dreumesdromen.nl

TOP E-TAILING TIPS:
- Let your business evolve naturally and don't rush. Be patient. It won't happen overnight – things take a while to get going.

- Take your time getting the design and appearance of your website right. It took me six months, working with a web designer, to get it looking how I wanted.

- Only sell products that you believe in.

- Don't set up an online shop to get rich – do it because you have a passion for something and you will never tire of running it.

THE FUTURE KEPT

www.thefuturekept.com

In the south of England, perched on a sleepy lane that winds across the verdant Sussex cliffs to a country park, is a pretty bungalow. The beach is a stone's throw away, so seagulls circle overhead and the air is salty and fresh. It is here that creative husband and wife Dean and Jeska Hearne live and work, running their new online boutique The Future Kept from their home office.

Dean and Jeska describe themselves as 'purveyors of well-designed, durable, meticulously chosen goods' and indeed they are; their pared-back virtual shop is filled with beautiful, honest items such as handmade wooden spoons, British lambswool blankets, natural vegan beauty products and artisanal gifts. 'We want to show that being eco-friendly can be chic and stylish,' says Jeska.

Their online and offline worlds overlap and merge, reflecting the design flair of the expert editors behind them. 'We only stock things that we personally like and would have in our own home,' explains Dean.

Both have creative backgrounds – Dean worked for a BMX distribution company and built up a brand importing and distributing bikes, while Jeska is an established style blogger – they took the plunge and set up shop together in autumn 2014.

'It's handy having our office close to hand, although it does mean we work strange hours sometimes,' says Jeska. 'Because we enjoy what we do, it doesn't really feel like work and we sometimes realize it's 9 pm and we're still at our desks!' Piles of stock fill their hallway and home office, but it's all immaculately organized and impressively tidy. 'Luckily, our products are lovely, so I don't mind having them lying around!' she adds.

When it comes to interiors, Jeska and Dean are resourceful and thrifty; their creativity and vision means their home is filled with interesting, eclectic finds that

ABOVE Jeska and Dean's creative home is filled with fascinating finds, picked up at car boot/yard sales, in junk shops or online. The teak rowing boat oars were a car boot/yard sale bargain, while the sideboard was 'reclaimed' from a pavement and 're-homed'. The couple's ability to see potential in the pieces others discard, combined with their flair for styling their home, means that they're able to elevate their serendipitous finds to new heights, displaying them in a way that enhances their beauty.

FACT FILE / THE FUTURE KEPT

CHIC BOUTIQUERS
Dean and Jeska Hearne

BASED
Hastings, UK

ONLINE SHOP
The Future Kept

ADDRESS
www.thefuturekept.com

LAUNCHED
2014

STOCK
Home and lifestyle accessories,
gifts and beauty products

SHOP STYLE
Edited, elegant, ethical

HOME
A cliff-top bungalow filled
with vintage finds – the couple
affectionately describe their
look as 'rescued chic'

STYLE TIP
No fireplace? Give
your room a focal point
with a piece of eye-catching
art and a centrally placed
sideboard or storage
unit for symmetry
and gravitas.

THIS PAGE The wall-hung whale was
made by a local artist and bought
in Butler's Emporium in Hastings.
'We won our armchairs on eBay and
had them covered in vintage fabric
from Wayward,' says Jeska.

somehow sit together seamlessly. Much of the furniture has been bought either from eBay or car boot/yard sales, while early morning runs along the coast give eagle-eyed Dean an opportunity to scout out local demolition projects, and he has sourced some great reclaimed items, such as free glazed doors, just by chatting to builders.

'We're always lucky when it comes to finding second-hand furniture on the street,' says Jeska, who 'rescued' their stunning teak G Plan sideboard after it was dumped on a pavement in Hastings. Now, it takes pride of place in their living room in front of a black-painted wall.

The plethora of vintage shops in nearby Rye and Hastings provide a rich hunting ground, too, and – from a £6 ($9) crate coffee table to a stylish Danish armchair – they've picked up some bargains over the years.

'Everything in our home has a story and bags of character,' says Dean, fondly. 'Some things just seem to want to live here! Whether our look is "on trend"

or not doesn't bother us. We just choose pieces we like that will last for a long time.'

Being creative, the couple often make things for their home, too. Jeska puts together evolving mood-boards for the walls, which she updates seasonally with inspiring prints and pictures, while talented carpenter Dean has fitted a bespoke clothes storage unit in the dressing room using reclaimed scaffolding planks and poles. It's affordable but incredibly sturdy and pleasingly industrial.

Car boot/yard sales provide plenty of plunder, too. 'We often go to local sales on Sundays with friends, and enjoy sifting through the junk – discarded old shoes and random tat – to find the gems,' says Dean. 'The vintage wooden rowing boat oars that lean against our living room wall were just £5.'

There's no TV in their home – instead, a friendly looking hand-painted whale decoration made by a local artist provides a quirky focal point on the wall. 'I hate

ABOVE FROM LEFT 'This is my chair,' says Dean. 'I've always wanted a chair like this. It needed a lot of work! We had it reupholstered in vintage fabric from Etsy.' 'Succulents are low maintenance,' says Jeska. 'We don't water them for weeks at a time. I love the shapes and textures.' Jeska compiles mood-boards around the house. 'Since I was 16 I've made scrapbooks. Now I use old frames I've painted and I just fill them with whatever I'm currently loving.'

'Our shop reflects how we choose to live our lives – being more considerate about how we consume items…'

the way that TVs dominate most homes,' says Jeska. 'We enjoy watching films on our laptop, but we sold our TV a while ago and we don't miss it at all.'

The couple's back-to-basics approach and their philosophy that simple and small is often better is echoed in all that they do. Driven by a desire for a better quality of life, and a belief that small, independent businesses can – and should – support one another, Dean and Jeska are passionate about an alternative way of living, steering clear of big brands wherever possible and relishing their role in an online, creative community of independent sellers.

'We have an authentic passion for what we do,' says Dean. 'Our shop reflects how we choose to live our lives

– being more considerate about how we consume items, what we choose to have in our own home, the companies we choose to support and work with; hopefully that authenticity shines through. It can be imitated, but it can't ever be done by a big brand or without true passion.'

Jeska agrees. 'I was in a big supermarket recently and I noticed that the store was selling coffee in little brown paper bags with labels that looked as though they'd been stamped by hand, to give the illusion of an artisanal, authentic product. I just thought: "No! Stop!".'

'When your store is your own and you're heavily invested in it personally, it helps your customers to have a stronger connection to it,' adds Dean.

OPPOSITE A few vintage crates and wooden planks form practical, temporary shelves in the living room, which Jeska fills with decorating books, cacti and pretty ornaments. She often uses these shelves as a set for styling products for The Future Kept.

THIS PAGE Dean and Jeska artfully arrange the objects in their home to create appealing still life vignettes – every surface is treated as an opportunity for display. The beautiful cob weave blanket is sold in their online shop and made in Wales.

THIS PAGE The couple's bedroom is filled with curiosities and vintage trinkets, picked up over the years. They have a knack for combining second-hand furniture with new finds and hand-crafted items. Jeska bought the metal leaf garland online and draped it over the curtain rail for a corner feature. Jewellery is stored on pretty hooks, while a shabby-chic bedside table adds character to the room.

OPPOSITE FROM LEFT The spare bedroom is currently used as a dressing room, where Jeska can store her collection of vintage clothes and jewellery; Dean has made a sturdy open storage unit from scaffolding poles and planks.

It's testament to their relationship that working together full time suits Dean and Jeska, who make the perfect team. While their roles overlap, each takes on defined responsibilities according to their contrasting strengths and weaknesses. Jeska styles the product shots and Dean takes the photos. Dean handles the technical side of the website, social media and marketing, whereas Jeska is in charge of the general aesthetics and overall look of the brand.

'We both know where we stand,' says Dean with a smile. 'Jeska packs the orders and I take them to the post office. She's better at wrapping than me – and I'm the one who can drive!'

Being a married couple can be an advantage when it comes to business. 'We have a shared vision,' explains Dean. 'Anyone who runs their own business knows it's really stressful. When you're passionate about something and you have a vision, those emotions are heightened – but even when it's a bit tense, we have the same end goal and share the same aesthetic. We never let our disagreements drag on.'

Jeska agrees: 'Because we're a couple, we can be honest with each other. Things that would be bottled up for years in another business are said instantly here – and sorted. We're quite different, which really helps.'

So, what does the future hold for this enterprising couple? 'We'd really like to design our own range of products and get some exclusive items made for us,' reveals Jeska. 'We'd also like a traveling, mobile shop of some sort one day – possibly in a 'rescued' van – to get out there and meet people in person,' she adds. It's clear Jeska and Dean's journey has only just begun…

THIS PAGE Jeska's desk has narrow shelves fitted above it, where she can display her vintage treasures. The letters 'L & S' stand for Lobster & Swan, Jeska's style blog. **OPPOSITE FROM TOP LEFT** The couple's home office is filled with traditional wrapping materials; nearby, 'gangster' cat Wallis oversees proceedings from her box in the corner; Jeska particularly relishes the simple, smaller tasks, such as hand-stamping luggage labels.

JESKA AND DEAN LOVE:
- Sparrow and Co.: www.sparrowandco.com
- Six and Sons: www.sixandsons.com
- Petit Pippin: www.petitpippin.com

TOP E-TAILING TIPS:
- Think carefully about why you want to set up a shop and write down your mission statement. This process could take a while, but it's important to get your ideas clear and focused, right from the start.

- Creating a good business plan is key, even if you don't intend to get a loan from a bank. It helps to fine-tune ideas and gives you an overall picture of your business, right from the start.

- Be realistic financially and don't get carried away – one of the advantages of setting up an online shop is that you can start small (we started The Future Kept with just a small amount of savings) and grow the business slowly.

OPPOSITE Asumi and Kuni found their yellow sofa and orange pouffe in a local second-hand shop. The elegant feather and leather decorations that hang on the wall are handmade by talented Asumi. The cushions are sold in Kanorado Shop.
RIGHT Neatly stacked wicker baskets contain spare linen and blankets in the couple's well-ordered home.
FAR RIGHT Navaho-inspired prints and small succulents give the living room a fashionable, fresh look – modest Asumi has her finger on the pulse when it comes to interior design trends.

KANORADO SHOP

www.kanoradoshop.com

Husband and wife team Kuni and Asumi Tomita have put together a meticulously edited selection of handmade and exclusive products for their online store Kanorado Shop. Like their online realm, their home channels an inspiring mixture of influences; their signature style is a beguiling combination of Japanese simplicity with a quirky, Brooklyn twist.

FACT FILE / KANORADO SHOP

CHIC BOUTIQUERS
Kuni and Asumi Tomita
BASED
New York, USA
ONLINE SHOP
Kanorado Shop
ADDRESS
www.kanoradoshop.com
LAUNCHED
2013

STOCK
Hand-crafted home and fashion accessories, with vintage finds
SHOP STYLE
Minimal, clean, handmade
HOME
A pre-war rented apartment in a townhouse in the Greenpoint area of Brooklyn

'Our lives and our shop merge together,' explains Asumi. 'We just share products and experiences that we love.'

ABOVE Asumi painted the dining table legs to match the walls. The colourful arrows on the wall were made by Brooklyn-based studio Fredericks & Mae. OPPOSITE Stacks of neat linens and orderly storage jars fill the kitchen shelves. 'I'm always rearranging the things on top,' says Asumi. 'At Christmas, I hung a wreath above as a focal point.'

Visiting Kanorado Shop always provides a restful hiatus in a busy day. The design is pared back and stunningly simple – all crisp white backgrounds, elegant fonts and inspiring photography. As you browse through the pages, you can't help but lose yourself in a world of beauty.

Part shop and part inspirational lifestyle resource, this impeccable website has a link to a separate 'photo journal' section hosted on Tumblr where Asumi and husband Kuni share photos of their travels, spent exploring remote, sanctuary-like places. It's completely enchanting and leaves you feeling more as if you're soaking up the pages of a hipster magazine than visiting a shop.

Both Kuni and Asumi grew up in Japan. 'We're from Tokyo,' says Asumi. 'I always loved art classes, but my parents advised me to go to a regular university and study a more academic subject, so I did English literature and cultural studies, focusing on the differences between Japanese and American leisure activites. My degree helped to broaden my horizons and when I left, I wanted to see more of the world.'

After graduating, Asumi still wanted to study design, so she came to New York in 2004 to do interior design at the Fashion Institute of Technology. She started working for a small residential interior design firm soon after. Kuni came to New York to study psychology, but his personal passion has always been photography, a skill he has inherited from his father.

Brought together by fate, Asumi and Kuni met through a mutual friend in 2007, got married in 2009 and soon realized that they made the

STYLE TIP
In a small kitchen, place a board on top of an open shelving unit, to create a surface that's perfect for displaying your favourite treasures.

perfect creative team. With Kuni's incredible photography skills and Asumi's eye for selecting beautiful objects and curating spaces (both real and virtual), the couple decided to set up shop together two years ago.

'We wanted to do something for ourselves,' explains Asumi. 'An online shop was the perfect solution, because we could both still work full time while we set it up – a bricks-and-mortar store costs a lot more to get running.'

They both still have day jobs. Kuni works on branding and photography for a Soho boutique called Makié, which sells beautiful children's clothes and womenswear, while Asumi spends two days a week in an interior design practice and the rest of her time helping the Brooklyn-based Coral & Tusk. Despite having two jobs and running an online shop, Asumi remains impressively unflustered. 'I enjoy the variation and find I focus on each role much better because I have limited time.'

The precision with which Kuni and Asumi have curated their store is admirable and many of their products cannot be found elsewhere. 'You have a much stronger identity if you sell things that nobody else does,' explains Asumi. 'Lots of shops look the same; it's much more interesting to sell things that only you have. If you can't find what you want, make it yourself.'

LEFT The flag above the bed is from Brimfield Antique Show. 'I think it's some sort of marine signal flag,' says Asumi. 'It's 100 years old.' The couple love the exposed brickwork, which is typical of Brooklyn homes. Their wedding photo takes pride of place on the bedside table.
OPPOSITE FROM LEFT The bent beech coat rail is the 'Tra-Ra Clothes Rail', designed by Tomoko Azumi (available at Heal's), a Japanese designer based in London; crisp cotton shirts hang on antique coat hangers, found on eBay; 'It's important to me to have greenery in the home,' says Asumi. 'I buy a lot of succulents for fresh air.'

This enterprising couple have invested time and energy in creating the very best designs they can, all handmade, built to last and effortlessly elegant. They bought crisp cotton fabric from a wholesaler and collaborated with a pattern-cutter and seamstress to create a collection of shirts. Asumi makes dainty hanging decorations herself, nimbly tying lengths of leather to delicate white feathers. They teamed up with a floral designer to put together a range of exclusive dried garlands. Weekends are spent scouring antiques fairs to find interesting vintage items to mix in with their new stock. The result is a shop that is a real one-off.

'Sourcing vintage items for the store at flea markets is something we love to do,' says Asumi. 'There's a huge fair in Massachusetts every summer – it's called the Brimfield Antique Show. We go there specifically to scout out stuff for the shop – and for our own home, too!' Indeed, the apartment Asumi and Kuni share has an interior that's peppered with vintage treasures, as well as handmade accessories and chic, Japanese elements.

The apartment is long and thin, with an open-plan kitchen-dining-living room at one end, a shared home office in the middle of the building and a bedroom at the other end. It's cosy, but uncluttered and, thanks to Asumi's interior design talents, it doesn't feel cramped. Her professional skills mean that every space is styled to perfection and she has the confidence to use bold hues that others might shy away from.

'I'm not afraid to use colour,' she says. 'Following a trip to California, we were really inspired by the amazing blue skies and seascapes we saw there. We wanted to paint a feature wall in a deep blue, to contrast with our yellow sofa and the bright orange pouffe.'

After trying a few samples, Asumi settled on the perfect paint – a rich, teal shade that provides both contrast and theatre. 'The walls were pale green before,' she recalls with a grimace. 'I don't hesitate to use strong shades for impact.' Asumi painted the legs of the dining table to match the wall. It's a small detail, but a genius move that ties the whole look together seamlessly. 'It was very easy to do,' she says, modestly.

It is this natural ability to create and curate beauty that sets Asumi and Kuni apart in a crowded marketplace, but what makes them so delightful is that somehow, despite their amazing achievements, they remain incredibly humble.

THIS PAGE The wrapping station in the couple's home office is a treasure trove of twine, luggage labels and ephemera. Small bouquets of feathers and dried flowers fill jars, while garlands by New York-based floral designer Eiko Fujii (available at Kanorado Shop) hang above. Asumi carefully wraps each order by hand.
OPPOSITE FROM TOP LEFT 'I like to keep lots of little bits and bobs to hand, so I can do lovely gift-wrapping,' says Asumi; business cards are kept in dainty leather bowls lined with floral fabric; a vintage marmalade jar is used as a pen pot, while an antique crate holds post/mail in the shared home office.

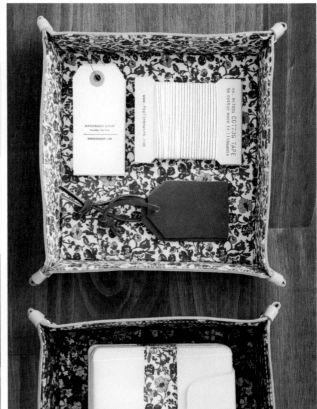

ASUMI AND KUNI LOVE:
• Makr: www.makr.com
• Quitokeeto: www.quitokeeto.com
• 20x200: www.20x200.com

TOP E-TAILING TIPS:
• Don't be afraid to get help. If you can, work with a graphic designer and web designer. It's like working with an interior designer for a real offline shop.

• When you're an online store, the packaging and the product are the only things that your customer sees in the physical world, so get them right. Careful wrapping represents your brand and leaves a good impression.

• Use a tool like MailChimp to send out email newsletters. You can see how many people click on links in the email, so you can gather information about how successful the email is and learn how to tailor your content accordingly.

LE SOUK

www.soukshop.com

Surrounded by open fields, flocks of geese and clusters of picture-perfect wood-clad houses is the village of Zuiderwoude, in the appropriately named 'Waterland' area, just north-east of Amsterdam. Here, blogger and boutiquer Danielle de Lange runs her online store Le Souk from an airy farmhouse that she and her husband Ivar have lovingly renovated, with stunning results.

FACT FILE / LE SOUK

CHIC BOUTIQUER
Danielle de Lange
BASED
Zuiderwoude, Netherlands
ONLINE SHOP
Le Souk
ADDRESS
www.soukshop.com
LAUNCHED
2008

STOCK
Handmade, beautiful homewares, jewellery and fashion accessories mostly from Turkey, Morocco and the Netherlands
SHOP STYLE
Scandinavian-meets-boho
HOME
A lofty, renovated 1920s farmhouse in an idyllic rural wetland setting

OPPOSITE FROM LEFT
'Natural materials
bring warmth,' explains
Danielle. 'We have lots
of white walls, which
can be harsh, so they
need to be balanced
with warmer woods.'
THIS PAGE Danielle bought
her second-hand Moooi
desk online. It was black,
but she had it spray-
painted white. The
vibrant kilim rug is
from Le Souk.

THIS PAGE & OPPOSITE Danielle's coffee table is from Indonesia. 'It's very rustic and sturdy – you can see it's part of a tree. That's what I like about it,' she says. The vintage rug is Moroccan. 'My look is a merging of Scandinavian style – clean lines and white – and natural materials and accessories that have an Asian and African influence. It's a global mix,' explains Danielle.

The most successful interiors are always those that are, in some way, perfectly balanced. So it is with Danielle de Lange's Netherlands home, which has a seamless blend of cool, clean Scandinavian chic and warm, eclectic, global style. Here, the key elements are simple and typically Dutch – there are oak floorboards, white walls and huge windows that let daylight flood in all year round. It's elegant and pared back, but never boring because the rooms are brought to life with textured, decorative accessories picked up on Danielle's travels to countries such as Turkey, Australia and Morocco, which combine to create a layered, welcoming look.

'Scandi' and 'boho' might be opposites, but the unlikely marriage of these two contrasting looks works like a dream, thanks to the superior styling skills of interiors-obsessed Danielle.

FAR LEFT Pared-back Scandi-chic ceramics and chunky, tactile wooden plates fill the kitchen dresser/hutch, neatly representing two contrasting strands that combine to create Danielle's personal style. LEFT A vintage crate is used in the kitchen to store olive oil, herbs and chopping boards, some of which are made by Dutch craftsmen at Brood & Plank, and are part of the selection of products that Danielle stocks.

'We bought this house in 2008. When it was originally built, it was a small working farm building,' says Danielle. 'The living room was once a stable block and the upstairs was a hay loft, but by the time we moved in, the previous owners had already converted the building into a family home.'

The work wasn't all done, however. Danielle and her husband Ivar embarked upon an enormous renovation, in order to open up the space and make the most of the incredible vistas the house enjoys.

'The house was in good shape, structurally, but it was a mess cosmetically,' she explains. 'It was dark, with small rooms, so we did a lot of work to open it up and make the home lighter.'

Now, the ground floor is mostly a large, open-plan living, dining and kitchen space, with glass doors to allow the spectacular view of the wetlands to be fully appreciated. 'I think open-plan living is great for family life, too,' says Danielle, who has a four-year-old son called Kick and a mischievous rescue dog named Lola with a penchant for chewing shoes. 'If Kick is drawing

at the table, I can be cooking in the kitchen but still chatting with him and keeping half an eye on Lola. It's sociable for entertaining, too, when we have friends over for dinner.'

The upstairs layout is equally impressive. Bedrooms and bathrooms – traditionally private, closed spaces – are refreshingly open plan throughout in this family home. 'We wanted to be able to see the lovely view from every room upstairs,' explains Danielle. 'That's why we don't have any doors in the bathroom area or in any of the rooms apart from the bedrooms, which we only close at night.'

A single, central walkway connects all the open spaces and this bold decision means that wherever you are, you can see straight through the house to the main bedroom window. In theory, you can lie in the bathtub at one end of the building and still admire the view on the opposite side of the house. It's very clever.

Danielle feels blessed to have the best of both worlds: 'We're so lucky to have nature all around us – every season is different and beautiful in a different way,' she says. 'In winter, the children go ice-skating on the waterways and in the summer they can play outside all day. Kick has his own vegetable garden and has friends whose parents are farmers, so he sees newborn animals and rides on tractors. It's a good life, but Amsterdam is only 15 minutes away, which is handy.'

It's important to Danielle that Kick has a rural upbringing. 'I read recently in a survey that, when city kids were asked what a cow looks like, they said 'it's purple' – because of the chocolate brand Milka's purple cow logo. It's so depressing!'

Danielle's career has been varied and, although she loved redecorating her bedroom when she was a teenager, she didn't immediately go into interior design. 'I studied French, German and English, then I went travelling – to New Zealand and Australia, worked as a flight attendant, then did a decade in the corporate world, but it was too "corporate" for me,' says Danielle, who has always been a creative at heart.

After doing a styling course, she enjoyed decorating homes for clients but hated deadlines and felt she was still 'missing something'. In 2006, she started her blog

BELOW 'In a kitchen, I like to have an island with stools, for socializing, and enough space for two people to cook and not feel cramped,' says Danielle. 'We wanted a custom-built kitchen with concrete, but it isn't very practical as it stains. In the end we opted for white and it's not a very unique kind of kitchen, yet it works well in this space.' Monochrome plates decorate the wall and neatly labelled jars of flour line the shelves.

RIGHT The star lamp in Kick's stylish but fun bedroom is by a Spanish firm called XO. Danielle has created a space that's child-friendly but also ultra chic. **FAR RIGHT** The teepee is from a French children's shop called Smallable. Danielle has placed a quilt underneath it and filled it with cushions to create a cosy den where Kick can read, play or nap.

– The Style Files – and discovered her true calling. 'I like being my own boss and having flexible hours,' she explains. 'In 2006, there were some blogs in the USA, but very few in Europe. It became my creative outlet.'

It wasn't long before Danielle began to be bombarded with questions about her home from readers. 'I got so many emails from people asking where they could buy the things they saw in the pictures of my home on my blog that I realized it made sense to open a shop.' In 2008, she took the plunge.

'The best bit about having a shop is scouring the globe for stock,' says Danielle, who loves to travel. 'I'm always looking for things for the shop

LEFT Kick's bedroom is a smart space that will suit his changing needs over the years. Rather than opting for a strong theme or colour scheme that he might grow out of, Danielle has kept the basics simple and added colour and fun with accessories.
OPPOSITE The incredible views through the bedroom window can be enjoyed from every room on the top floor thanks to open-plan living, a central corridor and a clever layout.

STYLE TIP
Make your bedroom feel serene with soft whites and creams, but include various textures to keep the look warm and welcoming.

and for my own home, and could happily spend every day of a holiday exploring markets.'

She is a great believer that an eclectic mix of personal finds is what makes a home interesting and unique. 'The things you find on your travels are what give your home a personal feel. Everything has a story and triggers a memory. If you just fill your home with new things from the high street, it's going to look boring.'

With aboriginal wall art, mid-century Indonesian chairs, Moroccan stools and vibrant, Turkish kilim rugs, Danielle's elegant home is certainly not boring. It's a characterful building, in a dream location, containing a carefully-edited collection of interesting finds, picked up all over the world. It's luxurious, but not fussy; comfortable, yet stylish. The perfect balance. Her shop aesthetic is the same – an online 'souk' where you can stroll at leisure, virtually travelling the globe, and you won't have to lug your finds back to the airport or pay 'excess baggage' fees.

'The things you find on your travels are what give your home a personal feel. Everything has a story and triggers a memory.'

ABOVE Natural wood plays an important role in Danielle's home, enriching cool spaces and bringing warmth to every room. The 'Coral' light pendant is by New Zealand designer David Trubridge. It's inspired by geometric polyhedra and is created from a single component that's repeated 60 times.
OPPOSITE FROM TOP Framed feathers bought in Amsterdam provide a simple but beautiful ornament and subtly reference the waterfowl that thrive in the fields surrounding the Danielle keeps her jewellery on show in glass display cases so that she can admire each piece; ornate hammam bowls are used to store soaps in Danielle's luxurious bathroom, giving the room an exotic, Moroccan ambiance; a rustic ladder is used to display and store clothes in Danielle's lofty dressing room.

DANIELLE LOVES:
• Humanoid: webshop.humanoid.nl
• Shak-Shuka: www.shak-shuka.com
• Bijzonder MOOI: www.bijzondermooi.com

TOP E-TAILING TIPS:
• Don't stock well-known, established brands because you can't offer the best prices – bigger shops can buy in bulk and offer lower prices.

• Think about your mark-up. I started by selling small, less-expensive things. But if you sell an item that's only 5 euros, you have to do the same work as you would for an item that's 100 euros. Business-wise, selling bigger items makes sense.

• It's important to put a handwritten thank-you card in with every order. I sell large items like rugs, which have to be wrapped practically, not prettily, but I always include a nice label and a note.

• You need to be good at managing your time – you always have less time to work than you think!

LAUNCH YOUR OWN
CHIC BOUTIQUE

HOW TO SET UP
AN ONLINE SHOP

Are you inspired by the beautiful homes and shops in this book? If you want to launch your own online store, but aren't sure where to start, soak up some expert advice from successful chic boutiquers first. You don't need to be an experienced entrepreneur or a clever website designer, thanks to templates and easy-to-use platforms; all you need is plenty of creativity, a brilliant idea, dedication and sheer hard work. Your research starts here…

'The brilliant thing about selling online is that it puts you into an enterprising mentality. An online shop is an instant marketplace that you can completely control in terms of the design and feel. You can tell stories through words and pictures, styled shots… you can make it an online destination and create a whole virtual world.'

KEITH STEPHENSON, MINI MODERNS

1. GET STARTED

WRITE A MISSION STATEMENT

Think carefully about why you want to set up a shop and write down your mission statement. This process could take a while, but it's important to get your ideas clear and focused, right from the start.

'First and foremost, spend time figuring out where you want to take your business and what your passion is. You need a mission statement. We wrote out what we wanted to achieve. It took a while to fine-tune it, but it's a document we refer to every time we make a decision, from what products we stock to how we want our business to be perceived.'
Dean Hearne, The Future Kept

PLAN YOUR FINANCES

If you want to secure investment or a loan from a bank, a business plan is crucial, but it's useful anyway, even if you're starting out very small scale, because it challenges you to put your ideas down on paper and makes the whole process seem much more real.

Governments provide free support and advice for small businesses, so tap into these resources. If you're based in the UK, you can find free downloadable business plan templates at www.gov.uk/write-business-plan. If you're based in the USA, refer to advice at: www.sba.gov/writing-business-plan.

'Be realistic financially and don't get carried away – one of the advantages of setting up an online shop is that you can start small and grow your business slowly. Get advice and help from your bank or an accountant if you need it.'
Jeska Hearne, The Future Kept

ASSESS YOUR SKILLS

Think about what your strengths and weaknesses are – what will you need help with? What can you already do? Make a list of your skills and areas you need to work on, perhaps with the help of others.

'If you run a small independent online shop, you have to do everything yourself. It's tough. You have to be an accountant, a social media expert, a website designer, a packer, a shipper, a marketing expert. We enjoy all these things, but it's hard work!'
Dean Hearne, The Future Kept

DO PLENTY OF RESEARCH

With a plethora of online shops out there, you need to ensure that yours stands out from the crowd. Get to know the market you'll be entering really thoroughly before you take the plunge and spend plenty of time considering what will make your shop different.

Visit as many online shop sites as you can and note down what you like and dislike about each one in terms of design, layout, stock, creative content, social media approaches and more practical elements such as shipping and delivery costs. Check out the competition and see what they do well.

Do some online shopping yourself and consider, as a customer, what your experience was like. What impressed you? How quickly did your order arrive? How was it packaged? Did you find it easy to interact with the shop owner online? The more you shop online yourself, the more you will learn and the easier it will be for you to work out what sort of customer experience you want to provide.

CHOOSE A GOOD NAME

Use www.instantdomainsearch.com to see if your shop website address is available and also check that the name you have chosen for your shop has not been used elsewhere on- or offline.

'Make sure that your name works fluidly across the internet – if somebody already has the handle you want on Pinterest or Instagram, choose a new name, one you can own completely. Keeping your brand and name consistent and strong across all platforms is essential.'
Dean Hearne, The Future Kept

2. CHOOSE A PLATFORM

Some of the chic boutiquers in this book pay for virtual 'space' online and have used a website designer to create a bespoke website for them, while others have chosen to use handy shop-hosting tools such as Etsy, Big Cartel and Shopify.

Having a bespoke shop website built for you by a designer is a way to get a completely personal design that reflects your brand. However, it is a pricey option

and, depending on the site design, you might need to pay your designer again in order to edit or update the site in the future.

Using a well-known online shop platform like Shopify, Etsy or Big Cartel means that you can set up a professional-looking shop yourself without any code or website design skills, for a low cost. You can also access and edit the site yourself, whenever you want.

It's important to put a lot of thought into where your shop will be hosted. Different platforms offer different tools and features, and prices vary.

'Research the various platforms carefully before you set up shop and ensure that the one you're signing up to will suit your needs. Online forums are a great place to find out information and ask questions in advance. You need the right tools to start your shop.'
Danielle de Lange, Le Souk

GET TO KNOW... BIG CARTEL

URL: www.bigcartel.com

USERS: Around 500,000 shopkeepers

CHIC BOUTIQUERS WHO USE BIG CARTEL: Sian Tucker, fforest general stores; Elaine Tian, Studio Joo; Kristina Dam, Kristina Dam Studio; Keith Stephenson and Mark Hampshire, Mini Moderns

PRICING AND PACKAGES

There are four packages to choose from. All fees are billed monthly. 'Gold' is Big Cartel's free package, which lets you sell up to five products (with one image of each product) for no fee. The next is 'Platinum', a 10-dollar package, which lets you sell up to 25 products, with five images of each product. The 20-dollar 'Diamond' package allows you to sell up to 50 products, with five images of each product. Big Cartel's 'Titanium' package is the most expensive but lets you sell up to 300 products, with five images per product.

KEY FEATURES

• Quick set-up – it's easy to upload your images, set prices and start trading in a matter of minutes.
• Big Cartel lets you track your inventory (not available with the 'Gold' package), so you can see at a glance exactly how many products you have sold and what you have left in stock. The system automatically marks products as 'sold out' when they're no longer available.
• You can sell in person using the Big Cartel iPhone app, so you can sell your stock in the 'real' world at fairs, events and markets if you wish.
• You can sell via Facebook using the 'Store' tab tool. It's easy to sell digital content such as videos, eBooks, music, photos and fonts using Big Cartel's integrated service Pulley (www.pulleyapp.com).
• You can fully manage your orders, download an order history, view order details, track which orders have and haven't been shipped, and even print packaging labels.

• Big Cartel comes with a checkout system, so your customers can easily pay using PayPal or Stripe, via credit card.
• A built-in statistics tool (not available with the 'Gold' package) lets you see how many visitors you're getting and how they're finding you – you can find out what websites and search terms are driving traffic to your shop. Big Cartel is also integrated with Google Analytics.
• Big Cartel shops are search-engine optimized, so customers can easily find you when they search the web.
• There's no need to use any code as the templates are ready-made, with customizable fonts, colours, themes and images.
• However, if you can (or if you have a designer who can), you can customize the site with JavaScript, CSS and HTML.
• If you want to, you can use discount code tools to promote your shop, or reward loyal customers.
• You can use any domain name you own to give your store a custom URL (not available with the 'Gold' package). For example, www.spoonmoon.bigcartel.com could simply become www.shop.spoonmoon.com.
• There are 'how-to' videos and step-by-step guides to help you run a successful business, plus the support team is available via email or Twitter Monday to Friday, 9am to 6pm (EST).

WHAT THE CHIC BOUTIQUERS SAY

'Big Cartel is so easy to use. I'd recommend it for beginners. You pay a tiny amount per month and as your shop grows, you can expand gradually. It's really easy to edit and update your shop – you can take a picture on your phone and upload it immediately, so you can run your shop on the go, wherever you are. The back-end is really easy to use and it has useful statistics so you can track your progress.'
Sian Tucker, fforest general stores

'Big Cartel is easy to use. The customer service is great, too. I have a lot more control over the look and feel of my shop on Big Cartel than on some other platforms. On Big Cartel, the branding is subtle. I briefly had an Etsy shop before I moved to Big Cartel. I think Etsy is amazing, but there is a lot of emphasis on social media and, because I am rarely at a computer, it wasn't quite the right fit for me.'
Elaine Tian, Studio Joo

'It is easy to set up and even change templates in Big Cartel and it is hooked up with PayPal, which is a safe way to shop all around the globe. I could imagine in the future I might move my shop from Big Cartel to a bespoke shop that is a part of my own website over time, but right now my online shop is mostly for people who live outside Denmark in countries where there aren't retailers stocking my products, so most of my transactions are to people abroad and the system suits me fine.'
Kristina Dam, Kristina Dam Studio

GET TO KNOW... SHOPIFY

URL: www.shopify.com

USERS: Around 160,000 shopkeepers

CHIC BOUTIQUERS WHO USE SHOPIFY: Helen Dealtry, Dealtry; Danielle de Lange, Le Souk; Jeska and Dean Hearne, The Future Kept

PRICING AND PACKAGES

• There are four packages to choose from. All fees are billed monthly.

• Shopify also takes a percentage of your total sale price.

• You can sign up for a free 14-day trial before committing to a package.

• The cheapest package is the 'Starter Plan', which costs around £10 ($15) per month and lets you sell up to 25 products.

• For £20 ($30) per month, you can sign up to the 'Basic' package, which allows you to sell an unlimited number of products, and gives you 1 GB of file storage.

• The 'Professional' package costs £55 ($85) per month, lets you sell an unlimited number of products and gives you 5GB of file storage plus extra features (see below).

• You can pay up to £125 ($190) per month for the 'Unlimited' package, which allows you to sell an unlimited number of products and gives you unlimited file storage plus lots of extra features (see below).

• The credit card rates vary according to what package you sign up to. If you have the 'Starter Plan' or 'Basic' packages, the credit card rate is 2.9 per cent plus a small flat fee of around 20p (30 cents) per transaction. The rate drops to 2.5 per cent plus fee if you have the 'Professional' package, and it goes down to 2.25 per cent plus fee if you sign up to the 'Unlimited' package.

KEY FEATURES

• Quick set-up, it's easy to upload your images, set prices and start trading in a matter of minutes.

• Shopify lets you track your inventory, so you can see at a glance exactly how many products you have sold and what you have left in stock. The system automatically marks products as 'sold out' when they're no longer available.

• You can sell in person by signing up to the Shopify POS (point-of-sale) software for laptop, iPhone and iPad app (extra fees apply), so you can sell your stock in the 'real' world at fairs, events and markets. You also get a free credit card reader. If you need to run a bigger, pop-up bricks-and-mortar shop, you can sign up for a retail package add-on for an extra £30 ($45), which lets you manage staff, print receipts and process split tender (part card and part cash) payments. In essence, this tool lets you turn iPads into cash registers and seamlessly sync your online shop with an offline shop.

• You can sell via Facebook – your 'fans' can buy products without leaving Facebook.

• It's easy to sell downloadable digital content such as videos, eBooks, music, photos and fonts directly.

• You can fully manage your orders, download an order history, view order details, track which orders have and haven't been shipped and even print packaging labels.

• Shopify comes with a checkout system, so your customers can easily pay using over 70 payment gateways, from Bitcoin to PayPal.

• Built-in analytics let you see how many visitors you're getting and how they're finding you – you can find out what websites and search terms are driving traffic to your shop. Shopify is also integrated with Google Analytics, so you can track sales, visits and referrals.

• Shopify shops are search-engine optimized, so customers can easily find you when they search the web.

• There's no need to use any code as the templates are ready-made, with customizable fonts, colours and themes.

• However, if you can (or if you have a designer who can), you can customize the site with CSS and HTML.

• If you want to, you can use discount code tools to promote your shop, or reward loyal customers. Choose from money off, percentage off or free shipping.

• You can use any domain name you own or purchase one through Shopify.

• You can run your Shopify shop from your phone, using Shopify Mobile.

• Customers can 'zoom' in on images and leave product reviews for approval.

• An 'export' tool lets you export your analytics reports for further analysis in spreadsheet software or so that you can send it to your accountant.

• Shopify is level-1 PCI compliant, so your customers' credit card data is safe.

• All Shopify shops offer social media integration, such as Pinterest, Instagram, Tumblr, Twitter and Facebook.

• Shopify integrates with apps like eCommHub, Ordoro and Inventory Source, so it's easy to set up a dropshipping business.

• There is an enormous online 'Shopify Manual' – a knowledge base filled with helpful tips to help you run a successful business, plus the support team is available via email, phone or live chat 24 hours a day, seven days a week. There is also a hub of 'Shopify Experts' – approved Ecommerce designers, marketing gurus and website developers, who you can hire to help you. The Shopify discussion forums are also packed full of advice.

• Whether or not you sign up to Shopify, you can access Shopify's online 'Ecommerce University', which is filled with case studies, expert advice and free guides covering everything from the legal side of setting up an online shop to crowd-funding, pop-up shops and content marketing. (See: ecommerce.shopify.com).

WHAT THE CHIC BOUTIQUERS SAY

'I like Shopify because it's user-friendly, but it's quite expensive because you pay a fixed fee every month, then a percentage of all the items you sell, plus fees for credit card processing, etc. It all adds up and lowers your profits, so you have to make sure your mark-up on your products will cover all these costs and still leave you with a bit!'
Danielle de Lange, Le Souk

'I'm not tech-savvy and I started with a basic template on Shopify. I soon felt I wanted extra features and a clearer design with better flow, so I have a more complex one now. It's still a work in progress because I have been doing the back-end myself. If I can do it, anyone could do it I would say! It took me a week to get it as I want it. Shopify is geared towards people who need more from a web shop – you can make it as complicated or as simple as you like. I like having control over my store myself, so for example, if my product list grows, I can easily add on extra items when I need to.'
Helen Dealtry, Dealtry

'We chose a template that we could customize with our own design so we could achieve the look we wanted.'

Dean Hearne, The Future Kept

GET TO KNOW... ETSY

URL: www.etsy.com

USERS: Etsy is a community of 30 million buyers and businesses. You can sell handmade goods, craft supplies and/or vintage items that are at least 20 years old.

CHIC BOUTIQUERS WHO USE ETSY: Maryanne Moodie

PRICING AND PACKAGES

• There are no membership fees.

• It costs 14 pence (22 cents) to list an item for four months, or until it sells.

• Once the item sells, Etsy collects 3.5 per cent of the sale price as a fee.

• Fees are accrued on a monthly bill, which Etsy emails to you at the end of the month. You must pay your bill by the 15th of the next month using PayPal or your credit card.

• You need a valid credit card to become an Etsy seller for verification purposes. Registration through PayPal is available as an alternative to credit card registration in certain countries.

KEY FEATURES

• The emphasis is on community – you can engage with shoppers, curators and makers to explore your passion.

• You can personalize the look of your shop by editing your profile, your product photos and your shop's landing page banner.

• Etsy has a 'Direct Checkout' payment system tool, which means buyers can pay with their credit or debit card in their local currency and you receive the funds in your bank account in your local currency. You can also accept PayPal, cheque or money order payments.

• You can engage with knowledgeable sellers and experts in 'Etsy Teams' (groups of like-minded sellers who share similar interests) and 'Online Labs' (live and archive 'how-to' videos from the Etsy admins).

• A 'Teams Fellowship Program' provides Etsy Teams with curated packages to help boost visibility, motivation and peer-to-peer learning via educational resources such as workshops, pop-up shops or craft shows, help with online promotional campaigns, leadership and community skill management. Etsy Teams can apply for the scheme online.

• Whether or not you sign up to Etsy, you can browse the Etsy online 'Seller Handbook' for great tips and advice about selling online. You'll find helpful articles on everything from shipping and legal structures to photography and marketing.

• Again, whether or not you are an Etsy seller, you can subscribe to 'Etsy Success' – a free email newsletter containing seller tips and resources. (You sign up by entering your email address when prompted on the 'Seller Handbook' page of Etsy.com).

• Editorial-style features such as 'Trending Items' and curated collections compiled by 'Community Tastemakers' make Etsy an online destination with creative content – your shop is part of a huge creative hub. Etsy asks bloggers and brands to choose their favourite buys.

• You can sell in person using the 'Sell on Etsy' app and card reader, which lets you process transactions and credit cards on your mobile device, so you can sell your stock in the 'real' world at fairs, events, pop-up shops and markets. Items sold in person get captured in your Etsy shop statistics and your online inventory adjusts in real time, even if buyers pay with cash. (The 'Sell on Etsy' card reader is only available in the USA at the moment, but Etsy has plans to expand this tool further afield soon.)

• Etsy runs an 'Etsy Affiliate' programme, where bloggers and website editors can earn commission on sales that result from featuring links to Etsy products and Etsy content on their third-party website.

• There are organized offline 'Etsy Labs' events around the world for Etsy sellers to attend in order to craft, learn and socialize with one another.

WHAT THE CHIC BOUTIQUER SAYS

'I love the way that Etsy supports small businesses that are owned and operated by individuals who are usually the primary producers. I love the fact that many of the sellers are women. Etsy has given me a successful platform for selling, creating community and connecting.'
Maryanne Moodie

OTHER ONLINE SHOP HOSTING PLATFORMS TO CONSIDER:

TEXTALK

URL: www.textalk.se/produkter/webshop
USED BY: Ylva Skarp

MIJNWEBWINKEL

URL: www.mijnwebwinkel.nl
USED BY: Janneke van Houtum, Liefs van Maantje

BIG COMMERCE

URL: www.bigcommerce.com

VOLUSION

URL: www.volusion.com

WOOCOMMERCE

URL: www.woothemes.com/woocommerce
(This is a free plug-in that lets you adapt a WordPress website and turn it into an ecommerce store.)

OTHER OPTIONS...

Many of the chic boutiquers in this book don't use a hosting platform with templates and tools; instead, they have bespoke websites that were designed for them. Asumi and Kuni Tomita of Kanorado Shop and Rebecca Uth of Ro Collection have taken this route.

WHAT THE CHIC BOUTIQUERS SAY

'Our site is a bespoke design. We didn't use a template, so we have complete control over how it looks. For example, if you hover over a product, the image enlarges – we couldn't find any templates that would let us do exactly what we wanted to do, design-wise.'
Asumi Tomita, Kanorado Shop

'I designed the Ro web shop myself. I knew exactly how it should look and worked with a good friend who did the design with me and a technician who did the programming. It's hosted on my own domain – we didn't use a template. It's very easy to update the website. It's based on a system called Ruby On Rails, an open-source web framework.'
Rebecca Uth, Ro Collection

3. SOURCE UNIQUE PRODUCTS

With thousands of online shops to choose from, not to mention some huge companies that stock millions of different items, you have to make sure that your stock will set you apart from the crowd.

Curating your product selection will probably be one of the more enjoyable, creative parts of running your online emporium, but it's vital to make sure that you sell things that either can't be found in many other places, or, if they can be found elsewhere, it's important to make them look better in your shop than they do in other shops.

deals and to build up relationships with your suppliers. If your shop has not yet launched, it's a good idea to show potential suppliers a preview of your site so that they can see exactly what sort of shop you will be running and you can show them how their products will be displayed.

'You have to meet people face to face and get to know them, conveying your concept to them. It's often best to do business in person. There are some makers in Portland, Oregon, who we wanted to work with, so Kuni went there to meet them and took a prepared presentation that showed each vendor how their product would be displayed in our shop, so they could fully understand our concept before we launched.'
Asumi Tomita, Kanorado Shop

'I source a lot of stock in Turkey and Morocco, and have built up relationships with people who sell, so I have a good network now.'
Danielle de Lange, Le Souk

'There are lots of similar online shops now – that's the problem with internet shopping. A savvy customer can shop around and find what they want at the cheapest price. There's a lot of competition, so don't stock well-known, established brands because you can't offer the best prices – bigger shops can buy in bulk and offer lower prices. You have to find your own niche and offer customers something unique instead.'
Danielle de Lange, Le Souk

'We sell lots of unique products and unusual, handmade items. We also sell knives, lanterns and enamel teapots which are available elsewhere, but we style them in our own way.'
Sian Tucker, fforest general stores

Just because you're selling online doesn't mean you can order all your goods online, too. Be prepared to network in the real world and haggle in person to get the best

4. GET THE DESIGN RIGHT

The chic boutiquers in this book have all put a lot of time and effort into creating beautiful homes, and their online realms are equally as stunning. With so many online shops, looks do matter and first impressions really count, so make sure that the design of your web shop reflects your brand and conveys your products in the best possible way.

'Use the best photos you can. That's the most important thing. Incredible work that's photographed badly gives people the wrong impression. It doesn't do your work justice if you put up a bad photo. Learn a few tricks – invest in some basic equipment and good photo-editing software, or hire a professional to help you. It makes such a difference.'
Elaine Tian, Studio Joo

'We used a graphic designer to achieve our goals. It's like working with an interior designer for a real offline shop. If you can visualize something in your mind, it's always best to ask professionals for help if you can, so they can help you make it happen.'
Asumi Tomita, Kanorado Shop

'Unfortunately, it's not enough to have good products. You have to present them in a really good way and it has to look professional all the way through. It's crucial to have good images. Not just for your web shop but for everything that you send out. There is so much competition out there, so you really need to find your own path and your own expression. It's how you can stand out from the crowd.'
Ylva Skarp

'I rented a basic website framework from a host, then asked a designer to help me develop a logo and a more personal site design. I came up with ideas and sketches and they did the technical programming, so we worked together to create it.'
Janneke van Houtum, Liefs van Maantje

'Refresh your look from time to time. The first version of my web shop looked outdated after a while, so it needed a makeover. The overall design is the first thing people see when they visit your online shop, so you have to make a good impression. Having a good, modern, fresh design is really important. Easy navigation is crucial, too.'
Danielle de Lange, Le Souk

'Make sure your site looks good on all devices and screens. You probably need a mobile version of your site as well as a desktop one. You've got to be on your game. Nobody has the time to bother messing around, so you need to make things as easy as possible for people.'
Helen Dealtry, Dealtry

5. GET SOCIAL

Growing an online business means using social media tools with confidence. If you're not comfortable using all the major platforms such as Pinterest, Twitter, Facebook and Instagram, arrange a lesson with somebody who is and brush up your skills as soon as possible.

Most online emporium owners say they benefit from having social media icons on product pages, to make sharing elsewhere easy for their customers, although a few boutiquers prefer to keep the design clean and simple without icons. It's a matter of personal choice.

While your main advantage as a small business is that you can share your personal story and the behind-the-scenes world of your online shop, remember that you are running a business and the overall impact needs to remain professional. Get the balance right – share but don't over-share. Don't treat your shop social media accounts in the same way that you would your personal accounts and make sure every post or update is 'on-brand'.

'Social media is really important. Too many people don't embrace it in the way that they should. Instagram is something we focus heavily on – it has a creative, inspiring community of users and it constantly challenges us and motivates us to do different things and move forward creatively. Relying on other people to promote your business won't ever work – they don't know it like you do. Do it yourself. With social media, pick one or two platforms and focus your energies on them.'
Jeska Hearne, The Future Kept

'When you're setting up your shop, consider what sort of brand you want to be. We are very personal, approachable and friendly as a brand, so we get involved heavily with social media. Otherwise, our brand values mean nothing. You have to act on what you stand for. You can't tell people you're funny –

you have to make them laugh! Our customers want to engage with us and they're loyal to us. We're online, but we want to interact. If Mini Moderns is a customer's destination, they naturally want to look at our Pinterest boards and interact with us on Facebook. It's quite depressing how big brands imitate small brands nowadays. When big companies employ somebody else to look after their Twitter account or Facebook page, etc, it makes me sceptical about a brand – it makes me feel a bit cheated! Nobody can really understand your brand like you do.'
Keith Stephenson, Mini Moderns

'I have a presence on all platforms but focus on Instagram the most – it's the perfect one for me. Making time for social media updates, which is almost a job in itself, can be tricky, but it's really important.'
Sian Tucker, fforest general stores

'Instagram is a great way of connecting with your customers so they can see the back-end of your business. It's important to use social media so that customers can form a relationship with you before they come to your store and after. Social media shows customers that your business is genuine, it's not fabricated – and it's usually a struggle! Being a small business and sharing your story – showing that you're human and that you've worked really hard to get where you are – is one of your strengths. Always include social sharing buttons on your product pages.'
Helen Dealtry, Dealtry

'Some people find it harder than others to "do" social media. Start with your friends and then they'll share your shop news with their friends. Alternatively, establish your social media accounts in advance and build up an online community before you launch. People like to see you being normal. Customers, especially women, like to relate to you and feel as if they know you. Be honest and be human.

That's your super-power as a small business owner. Big companies can't show warts and all. When it's just you creating stuff, you can share your highs and lows – this is what makes you real.'
Maryanne Moodie

'We don't do Facebook because it doesn't justify the design of our brand. We focus more on Instagram, blogs and Pinterest. Online publicity is great as people can quickly click on a link and they get taken immediately to your site to shop, whereas in print media, people have to take the time to type your shop name into Google and find you. We don't have social media icons on our site because we prefer a less cluttered look. We find people "pin" our photos anyway.'
Asumi Tomita, Kanorado Shop

'I have 16,000 followers on Instagram. It really helps my business. I was against social media to start with and didn't feel as though I had the time, but Instagram is quick and it's all about the image – you don't have to write a lot of text, which suits me fine. You have to decide what to share. I want my social media updates to be personal but not private, so I never show pictures of my family. It's strictly business. I share pictures of my home – they always get the most "likes" by far! It's a good way to show my products in a home setting and give customers ideas of how my designs look in a real home.

'It's good not to be too eager. Be selective. Some days I don't post anything and some days I post twice. If you're posting too much, people might get sick of it. You should try to do it with joy and don't feel pressurized to do loads of updates.

'When somebody looks at your Instagram stream, there should be a flow and a cohesive look to your images. Take photos and edit them in a similar way, so you have a strong identity and the whole page looks good.'
Ylva Skarp

6. PLAN YOUR MARKETING AND PR

Keep a database of customers and keep in touch with them regularly (but not too often!) using email newsletters. You can include a 'sign-up' feature on your website so that shoppers can subscribe to your updates. Tools such as MailChimp make sending out marketing material to your customers much quicker and easier.

'MailChimp is a useful tool for sending out email newsletters – it does a lot of the hard work for you. You can write the newsletter when you have time and schedule it to send on a future date.'
Helen Dealtry, Dealtry

'We use MailChimp software to send out our newsletters. You can see how many people click on links in the email, so you can gather information about how successful the email is and learn how to tailor your content to your audience.'
Asumi Tomita, Kanorado Shop

If you don't have the budget to hire a professional agency, which can be pricey, it's crucial to invest time and energy into learning how to do your own PR, too, to attract new customers to your shop. Follow these steps to ensure your products get featured online on blogs and websites, as well as in traditional print media outlets such as magazines and newspapers.

TIME YOUR PR PERFECTLY

Be aware of lead times. Most monthly consumer magazines work four to six months in advance, so editorial teams work on Christmas features in the summer. That said, while newspapers and weekly magazines have much shorter lead times, online publishers probably don't have much lead time at all. So make sure you time your media releases appropriately. You should send press releases out in three batches – long lead, short lead and online.

TARGET THE RIGHT PEOPLE

Create a list of journalists on Twitter and study their tweets each day to see what they're looking for or working on. Social media can be hard work, but it opens up a whole new way to contact members of the media and get their attention.

Contact specific journalists. Do your research – buy a copy of the magazine or paper, or browse the website you are targeting and make a list of who writes the pages you want to get your products on. Contact details for all staff journalists are usually listed in the publication somewhere, or you can telephone the office number to find out who's best to contact. Send emails to individuals rather than to general addresses and, for posted press releases, address envelopes with correctly spelled names and up-to-date job titles. It doesn't hurt to send a physical, printed press release as well as emailing a digital version. Different journalists work in different ways and you want to cover all bases. Make sure you put the correct name and magazine or website title in the email content if you are doing lots of copying and pasting. It's time-consuming, but if you buy a magazine, go through every page and look for the credits on every feature – you'll be surprised by how many freelance journalists are involved. Make a list of their names, search for them online and create a database of who works for who. Don't just target staff writers – target freelance writers, too.

DON'T FORGET STYLISTS

If you are happy to loan your products for photo shoots, target the stylists and decorating editors and make them aware of your products. When you send in a sample, have a pre-prepared loan form for the stylist to sign and send back to you, setting out the terms of the loan and agreeing to pay for any lost or damaged stock, so that you can easily invoice if your sample is lost. Always include a printed, adhesive return address label, too, to make returning your stock simple.

KEEP IT SHORT AND SWEET

Journalists have hundreds of emails to wade through every day, so limit yourself to a few lines introducing your company and what your newest or best-selling products are. Attach a few low-resolution images, but don't include large high-resolution image files at this stage, as it clogs up the recipient's inbox and your message could even go straight to their junk mail folder if it's too large. A link to an online download site where images are stored is much better. The same goes for a printed press release. A journalist just wants to know the basic facts and to see a few examples of what you sell. Remember to include your contact information clearly.

HAVE PRESS-READY PHOTOS PREPARED

Your online shop is the perfect place to get creative and style some gorgeous lifestyle shots in settings to make your products look lovely, but some journalists and bloggers will just require a high-resolution 'cut-out' image of a product on a white background. You may not want to show blank background images in your shop, but take the trouble to shoot every item you sell individually on a white background (a plain, flat bed sheet or a big white piece of paper does the trick) with a good-quality digital camera and keep these simple 'cut-out' images to hand somewhere so that you can email them across quickly if a journalist or blogger requests one.

If you're tech-savvy you could 'cut the products out' yourself using Photoshop or Pixlr software (there are tutorials on YouTube), but most publishing companies just need a simple image with no background interference for them to cut out professionally at their end. Often, journalists are working to a tight deadline and won't have time to call in a sample from you and shoot it themselves on a white background in a studio, so being prepared with these high-resolution cut-out images is a must. Make it clear on your press release that you can supply high-resolution, at least 300dpi (dots per inch), cut-out images as well as high-resolution versions of the lifestyle images visible on your page.

MAKE SURE YOU'RE AVAILABLE

Ensure that you can answer emails and take phone calls every day. A journalist on a deadline isn't going to have time to call you several times – they will simply find another product from another stockist. Similarly, if a journalist wants to borrow a product for a photo shoot, make it as easy as possible. Send it by first-class post/mail or next-day delivery, and enclose a label with the return address written clearly on it.

KEEP IN TOUCH

Keep journalists and bloggers informed with your news, but don't bombard them every week or every time you introduce a new product to your shop. A phone call or an email now and again is great, but two or three a week is too much.

BE PREPARED

If your products are being featured on a big blog or in a magazine, ensure you are ready for an influx of orders!

'If you have a big media push coming your way, make sure you have enough inventory so you're ready.'
Helen Dealtry, Dealtry

7. MAKE YOUR PACKAGING PERSONAL

One of your strengths as a small business is to ensure that every item you send out conveys the right message, impresses your customers and reminds them that they are supporting a small business that has plenty of character compared to a faceless international brand.

'Our products are special things, so we want them to look special when they arrive, like a present. I love beautiful packaging. It would be easy to grab an item, stick it in a box and throw it out of the door, but if somebody takes the time to place an order with us, we want to give them respect back, so we take pleasure in putting time and care into the items they receive.'
Jeska Hearne, The Future Kept

'Things do get broken in transit sometimes, but you learn which carriers are a bit more careful with your products. Now, I tend to double-box everything and use a lot of packaging materials. I have had boxes come back to me that look as if an elephant has trampled on them!'
Elaine Tian, Studio Joo

'Even if they don't select a gift-wrap option, people love to receive carefully and beautifully wrapped items. We enjoy putting time and effort into our packaging.'
Asumi Tomita, Kanorado Shop

'I always put a hand written thank-you note in with packages. It's another way you can stand out. It's important to me that things feel personal even though my business is growing bigger. My employee and I wrap and send out everything ourselves.'
Ylva Skarp

'I often sell large items like rugs, which have to be wrapped practically, not prettily, but I always include a nice label and a handwritten note. Sometimes when I order something online myself, I get a package and there's confetti, balloons and candy inside and so on – I don't think these extras are necessary and it seems a bit wasteful as it all just ends up in the bin! I prefer a well-wrapped package that's professional and smart. Packaging has a job to do, but it doesn't have to be shiny or very heavy. I like practical, eco-friendly packaging.'
Danielle de Lange, Le Souk

'Our packaging is basic but beautiful – cardboard, brown paper and string. Packaging should be inkeeping with your brand.'
Sian Tucker, fforest general stores

8. HAVE A PRESENCE IN THE OFFLINE WORLD

Although your shop is online, mingling with customers face to face in the 'real' world when you can is crucial, too. Organize events such as studio sales, pop-up shops and workshops, and build customer loyalty as you expand your network.

'We love having studio sales and meeting our customers face to face. Doing pop-up shops gives you a chance to step back and see the overall picture – when all your stock is out in one place. You can see where you've been, where you are and where you're going. It helps us to make decisions about colours and so on.'
Mark Hampshire, Mini Moderns

'In Melbourne, I once put a huge loom in the window of a florist's shop and chose yarns that matched the colours of the seasonal flowers. I sat in the window for a week and we spread the word on social media – lots of people popped in to have a go. The combination of weaving and community hit all the right spots.'
Maryanne Moodie

9. BECOME A MULTI-TASKER

Running your own online shop means you need to become an expert at time management. You'll have orders to ship, emails to answer, packaging materials to buy, products to order, financial records to update, images to edit, photos to take, press releases to send out, social media posts to publish – it's difficult to multi-task. Plan your schedule carefully and, despite being available via email 24 hours a day, try to have some time off when you're 'offline' so that you don't burn yourself out.

'The hard part of running your own business is juggling all the different responsibilities. PR, management, creative work – I am probably at the stage where I need somebody else to help me. I have lots of things to deal with at once. I want to be the creative one and sometimes it feels like all I'm doing is running a business. It's a struggle sometimes. I have to remind myself that it's a good sign and being so busy means that the business is growing.'
Ylva Skarp

'Sometimes, you can't do everything. For your own sanity, you have to have a schedule of some sort. For example, you might reply to emails and queries on Monday mornings, for four hours. I'm learning to prioritize and compartmentalize. You can't do everything. Shipping, packing, mailing, social media, updating the website, changing your imagery, marketing, PR, shoots, look books, photography – it's a job that involves many jobs!'
Helen Dealtry, Dealtry

'When you run your own small business, you're not like Amazon.com! I'm a one-woman show and try to respond to customers within 24 hours, but some people can be demanding and expect you to be instantly responding to them like a bigger firm can.'
Danielle de Lange, Le Souk

10. ALWAYS FOLLOW YOUR HEART

Setting up an online shop is a labour-intensive, stressful process, but it should be an enjoyable, fulfilling one, too. If you're motivated by money alone, chances are you will get fed up of the whole thing pretty quickly. If you have a passion for what you do, however, and you're able to use your shop as a creative outlet, then luck might well be on your side.

'You need time, patience and passion. You shouldn't start an online shop to get rich – you should be driven by a love for what you do. Enjoy the process of putting it together and compiling your stock. Let your shop comfortably evolve. My store is gradually growing. Three years ago I couldn't imagine doing this. It's all a learning process. Enjoy what you do and do it with love. That's the most important thing. Only sell products you believe in, not for commercial reasons.'
Janneke van Houtum, Liefs van Maantje

'If you have a passion or a vision, or a strong idea, that's what's going to get you through the hard times. If you just want to make money, there are probably much easier and less stressful ways of making money! If you're just chasing money, you won't have passion for it and it won't work. Do it for the lifestyle it offers you and the creative options – we love shooting photos and social media. You have got to enjoy what you're doing, or what's the point?'
Dean Hearne, The Future Kept

GLOSSARY

CSS

Cascading Style Sheets is a simple style sheet language used to add style such as colours, fonts and spacing to web documents.

DOMAIN

The web address of your website or online shop.

DPI

Dots per inch is a measure of dot density in a digital image when it is reproduced in the real world, for example, printed out on paper. The higher the dpi value, the better quality the image will be when printed. The larger the image is to be printed, the higher the dpi value will need to be in order to avoid a pixilated look.

GOOGLE ANALYTICS

A web analytics tool from Google that lets you see important information about who is visiting your online shop, such as how many visitors your shop gets every day, how they arrived at your site (via email, social media or a search engine search) and where they are geographically in the world.

HOSTING

The virtual space that you 'rent' on the internet, where your website or shop is stored.

HTML

HyperText Markup Language is the basic code used for programming websites to give them structure.

ICONS

Small logo image buttons that represent social media sites or apps.

JAVASCRIPT

The programming language of HTML and the web.

PLATFORM

An online tool that provides virtual space and templates for you to run your shop. Also known as a hosting platform.

PR

Public relations is the way that businesses communicate with the media and the general public in order to create and maintain a positive image.

RESOLUTION

This refers to the detail that an image holds and is often discussed in terms of 'dots per inch'. An image with a 'high' resolution (300dpi or above) has more detail than an image with a 'low' resolution (72dpi or below).

SEARCH ENGINE

A tool such as Google, that searches content on the internet for you.

SEO

Search engine optimization refers to methods you can implement to ensure that your online shop ranks highly in search engine listings, maximizing traffic.

SOCIAL MEDIA

Services such as blogs, Twitter, Facebook, Google+, Pinterest and Instagram that allow users to interact, chat, network and share images and ideas.

URL

Uniform resource locator means the web address of a website, such as www.minimoderns.com.

SOURCES

1STDIBS
Stockists of antique furniture, fine art, costume jewellery and more.
www.1stdibs.com

20X200
Limited edition contemporary prints.
www.20x200.com

&TRADITION
Nordic furniture and lighting made from natural raw materials.
www.andtradition.com

AARSTIDERNE
Organic vegetable box delivery.
www.aarstiderne.com

ABC CARPET & HOME
Furniture, antiques, textiles and accessories from around the world.
www.abchome.com

ADAM DANT
Artworks that chronicle London life.
www.tagfinearts.com/adam-dant.html

ARNE JACOBSEN
Architectural and design resource.
www.arne-jacobsen.com

BAILEY DOESN'T BARK
Handmade ceramics.
www.bdbny.com

BLANCA GÓMEZ
Contemporary prints in various sizes.
www.etsy.com/uk/shop/blancucha

BIJZONDER MOOI
Stockist of Dutch accessories, gift and stationery designs.
www.bijzondermooi.com

BLU DOT
Minneapolis-based furniture design.
www.bludot.com

BRIMFIELD ANTIQUE SHOW
Huge outdoor antiques fair.
www.brimfieldshow.org

BROOD + PLANK
Traditional Dutch cutting boards.
www.broodenplank.nl

BROOKLYN FLEA
Flea market open at weekends April–November.
www.brooklynflea.com

BUTLER'S EMPORIUM
Vintage shop in Hastings, UK.
www.butlersemporium.com

BY LASSEN
Danish furniture and accessories.
www.bylassen.com

CASTIGLIONI
Italian lighting design.
www.fondazioneachillecastiglioni.it

CINNOBER SHOP
Independent bookshop in Copenhagen selling design, illustration and art books.
www.cinnobershop.dk

CORAL & TUSK
Embroidered and embellished textile designs.
www.coralandtusk.com

DAVID TRUBRIDGE
Lighting and seating designs.
www.davidtrubridge.com

DESIGN WITHIN REACH
Online stockist of furniture, lighting and accessories.
www.dwr.com

DREUMES DROMEN
Wall hangings and decorative items.
www.dreumesdromen.nl

EBAY
Online marketplace for individuals and businesses.
www.ebay.com

EIKO FUJII
Floral designer based in New York.
www.eikofujii.com

ELKELAND
Danish wall-hanging designer.
www.elkeland.bigcartel.com

ELLEN GIGGENBACH
Illustrator and surface designer.
www.ellengiggenbach.com

ETSY
Online marketplace for businesses.
www.etsy.com

FEARS AND KHAN
Online shop for furniture, lighting, posters and paintings.
www.fearsandkahn.co.uk

FERM LIVING
Decorative accessories, wallpaper, textiles and stationery.
www.fermliving.com

FLOS
Bespoke light solutions company.
www.flos.com

FREDERICKS & MAE
Kites, games and decorative utensils.
www.fredericksandmae.com

G PLAN
Designer seating solutions.
www.gplan.co.uk

GAIA & GINO
Contemporary lighting and glassware with Turkish influence.
www.gaiagino.com

GEORG JENSEN
Luxury jewellery, watches, cutlery/flatware and other silverware.
www.georgjensen.com

GRANIT
Collapsible seating, luxury camping gear, storage solutions and fabric accessories.
www.granit.com

HACHET + BEAR
Handcrafted spoons, utensils and other useful objects.
www.hatchetandbear.co.uk

HANS WEGNER
Chairs, tables and office furniture.
www.carlhansen.com

HARRIS TWEED
Accredited weaver of Harris Tweed.
www.harristweed.org

HAY
Innovative but classic design store with contemporary Danish items.
www.hay.dk

HEAL'S
Homewares store in the UK and online.
www.heals.com

HENRYBUILT
Bespoke kitchen and household system solutions.
www.henrybuilt.com

HOPPER AND SPACE
Modern chairs, lighting and accessories.
www.hopperandspace.com

HUMANOID
Clothing, shoes and accessories.
webshop.humanoid.nl

IKEA
Swedish furniture supplier.
www.ikea.com

LEANDER
Baby and children's room furniture.
www.leander.com

LONDON TRANSPORT MUSEUM SHOP
Wide range of posters, clothes, toys and chic homewares.
www.ltmuseumshop.co.uk

MAKIÉ
Clothes, homewares and jewellery.
www.makieclothier.com

MAKR
Leather and wooden luggage, belts, furniture and hard goods.
www.makr.com

THE MINIMALIST
Prints, frames, light boxes and other furniture and lighting.
www.theminimalist.com.au

MODERN MANOR STORE
Furniture, design and staging rentals.
www.modernmanorstore.com

MOOOI
Online homewares store based in The Netherlands
www.moooi.com

MUUTO
Scandinavian furniture and lighting designs.
www.muuto.com

NINA INVORM
Ceramics featuring illustrations.
www.etsy.com/nl/shop/ninainvorm

ORGANIC MAKERS
Organic skincare and cosmetic products free from synthetics.
www.organicmakers.se

PADDLE8
Marketplace for art collectors.
www.paddle8.com

PETIT PIPPIN
Handmade soft toys and art prints.
www.petitpippin.com

THE POSTER CLUB
International webshop selling posters.
www.theposterclub.com

POUL KJÆRHOLM
Mid-century furniture designer.
Available at:
www.fritzhansen.com

PRESENT AND CORRECT
Stationery designs and online shop.
www.presentandcorrect.com

QUITOKEETO
Knives, candles and kitchen tools.
www.quitokeeto.com

RICE
Danish homewares and accessories in melamine, glazed ceramic and handmade wicker.
www.rice.dk

RUM21
Interior design store selling everything from ceramics to lighting, fixings and furniture.
www.rum21.se

RYO KUMAZAKI OF STUDIO NEWWORK
Graphic design studio in New York.
www.studionewwork.com

SHAK SHUKA
Eco-friendly family items and children's clothing.
www.shak-shuka.com

SIX AND SONS
Online vintage store with Amsterdam retail space.
www.sixandsons.com

SPARK DESIGN SPACE
Design gallery in Reykjavík
www.sparkdesignspace.com

SPARTAN SHOP
Beautiful, practical objects in marble, metal, ceramic and fabric.
www.spartan-shop.com

SPARROW AND CO
Homewares collection by Samuel Sparrow.
www.sparrowandco.com

SMALLABLE
Online children's department store.
www.smallable.com

SUGRU
Mouldable and removable glue.
www.sugru.com

TOMOKO AZUMI
Multi-cultural design team based in East London, led by Tomoko Azumi.

TOTOKAELO
Purveyor of fashion and objects.
www.totokaelo.com

VICTOR WANG
Fine artist and professor of fine arts.
www.victorwang.net

VINTAGE MARTINI
Vintage clothing retailer.
www.vintagemartini.com

WAYWARD
Large quantities of vintage haberdashery items.
www.wayward.co

WHITE TRASH
Specialist mid-century modern furnishing dealer.
www.whitetrashnyc.com

XO-IN MY ROOM
Upcycled furniture retailer.
shop.xo-inmyroom.com

PICTURE CREDITS

All photography by James Gardiner.

1 The Brooklyn home of Asumi & Kuni Tomita of Kanorado Shop; 2–3 The Brooklyn home of Helen Dealtry of wokinggirldesigns.com; 4 left Ylva Skarp ylvaskarp.se; 4 centre The Brooklyn home of Helen Dealtry of wokinggirldesigns.com; 4 right Jeska and Dean Hearne thefuturekept.com; 5 left The family home of Danielle de Lange of online shop Le Souk soukshop.com and lifestyle blog The Style Files style-files.com; 5 centre Jeska and Dean Hearne thefuturekept.com; 5 right The Brooklyn home of Asumi & Kuni Tomita of Kanorado Shop; 7 left Jeska and Dean Hearne thefuturekept.com; 7 right The Brooklyn home of Asumi & Kuni Tomita of Kanorado Shop; 8–19 Mark Hampshire and Keith Stephenson of Mini Moderns; 20–29 Kristina Dam Studio; 30–39 The Brooklyn home of Helen Dealtry of wokinggirldesigns.com; 40–49 Rebecca Uth, creator of Ro; 50–61 Ylva Skarp ylvaskarp.se; 62–71 Maryanne Moodie; 72–81 Elaine Tian of Studio Joo; 82–93 The home of James Lynch and Sian Tucker of fforset.bigcartel.com and coldatnight.co.uk; 94–103 The family home of Janneke van Houtum of liefsvanmaantje.nl in Eindhoven; 104–113 Jeska and Dean Hearne thefuturekept.com; 114–121 The Brooklyn home of Asumi & Kuni Tomita of Kanorado Shop; 122–131 The family home of Danielle de Lange of online shop Le Souk soukshop.com and lifestyle blog The Style Files style-files.com; 132–133 Ylva Skarp ylvaskarp.se; 134 Elaine Tian of Studio Joo; 135 The family home of Danielle de Lange of online shop Le Souk soukshop.com and lifestyle blog The Style Files style-files.com; 137 The home of James Lynch and Sian Tucker of fforset.bigcartel.com and coldatnight.co.uk; 143 above left The Brooklyn home of Asumi & Kuni Tomita of Kanorado Shop; 143 above right The home of James Lynch and Sian Tucker of fforset.bigcartel.com and coldatnight.co.uk; 143 below left Maryanne Moodie; 143 below right The family home of Janneke van Houtum of liefsvanmaantje.nl in Eindhoven; 144 Elaine Tian of Studio Joo; 147 Mark Hampshire and Keith Stephenson of Mini Moderns; 148 Elaine Tian of Studio Joo; 150 The Brooklyn home of Asumi & Kuni Tomita of Kanorado Shop; 151 Rebecca Uth, creator of Ro; 153 The Brooklyn home of Helen Dealtry of wokinggirldesigns.com; 157 Ylva Skarp ylvaskarp.se; 160 Rebecca Uth, creator of Ro.

BUSINESS CREDITS

ELLIE TENNANT
Interiors journalist, stylist
and author
+44 (0) 7815 869370
ellie@ellietennant.com
www.ellietennant.com

DEALTRY
Helen Dealtry
2–3, 4 centre, 30–39, 153.
www.helendealtry.com and
Woking Girl Designs LLC
info@wokinggirldesigns.com
www.wokinggirldesigns.com

FFOREST GENERAL STORES
James Lynch and Sian Tucker
82–93, 137,143 above right.
info@coldatnight.co.uk
www.fforest.bigcartel.com
and www.coldatnight.co.uk

THE FUTURE KEPT
Jeska and Dean Hearne
4 right, 5 centre, 7 left,
104–113.
hello@thefuturekept.com
www.thefuturekept.com

KANORADO SHOP
Asumi and Kuni Tomita
1, 5 right, 7 right, 114–121,
143, 150.
inquiry@kanoradoshop.com
www.kanoradoshop.com

KRISTINA DAM STUDIO
Kristina Dam
20–29.
info@kristinadam.dk
www.kristinadam.dk

LE SOUK
Danielle de Lange
5 left, 122–131, 135.
www.soukshop.com and
Lifestyle blog 'The Style Files'
www.style-files.com

LIEFS VAN MAANTJE
Janneke van Houtum
94–103, 143 below right.
www.liefsvanmaantje.nl

MARYANNE MOODIE
Maryanne Moodie
62–71, 143 below left.
hello@maryannemoodie.com
www.maryannemoodie.com

MINI MODERNS
Mark Hampshire and
Keith Stephenson
8–19, 147.
www.minimoderns.com

RO COLLECTION
Rebecca Uth
40–49, 151, 160.
ro@rocollection.dk
www.rocollection.dk

STUDIO JOO
Elaine Tian
72–81,134, 144, 148.
www.studiojoo.com

YLVA SKARP
Ylva Skarp
4 left, 50–61, 132–133, 157.
info@ylvaskarp.se
www.ylvaskarp.se